INSPIRATIONAL CLASSICS

ISBN-13: 978-1-4234-2216-7
ISBN-10: 1-4234-2216-3

HAL•LEONARD®
CORPORATION

7777 W. BLUEMOUND RD. P.O. BOX 13819 MILWAUKEE, WI 53213

Visit Hal Leonard Online at
www.halleonard.com

ALWAYS THERE

Words and Music by BRENDAN GRAHAM
and ROLF LOVLAND

Warmly

When I'm less than ___ I should be, ___ when I
brings me ___ to my knees, ___ when my

just can't face the day, ___ when dark-ness ___ falls a-
back's a-gainst the wall, ___ you are stand-ing ___ there right

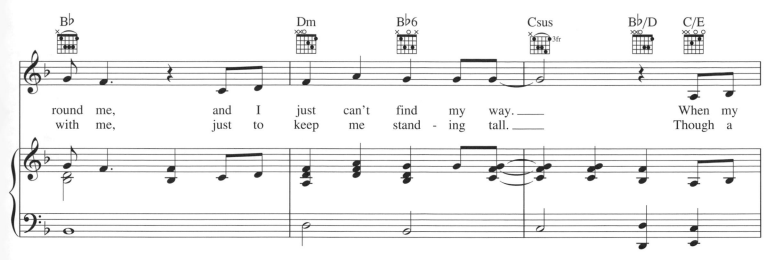

round me,   and I just can't find my way.____   When my
with me,   just to keep me stand - ing tall.____   Though a

eyes don't clear - ly see,____   when I stum - ble ____ through it all, ____
bur - den I ____ may be,____   you don't wea - ry, ____ you don't rest. ____

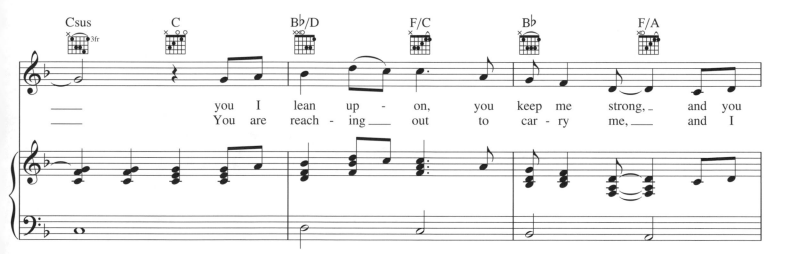

____   you I lean up - on, you keep me strong, __ and you
____   You are reach - ing ____ out to car - ry me, ____ and I

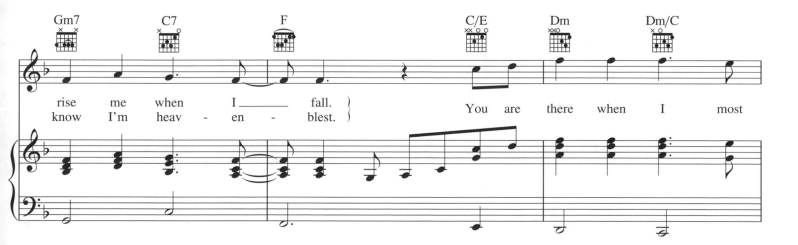

rise me when I _____ fall. }   You are there when I most
know I'm heav - en - blest. }

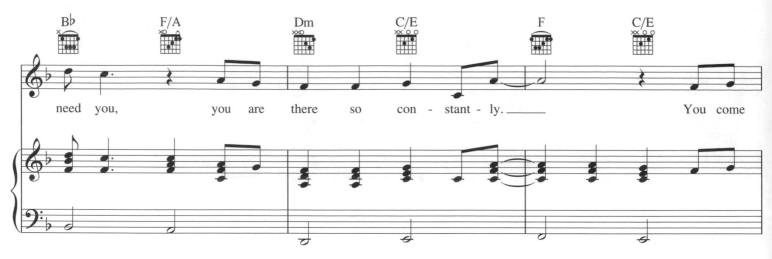

need you, you are there so con- stant- ly. _____ You come

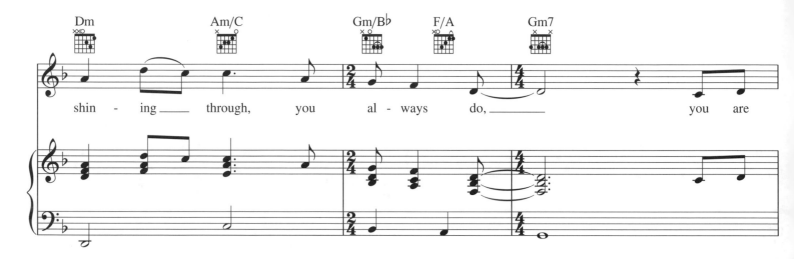

shin - ing _____ through, you al - ways do, _____ you are

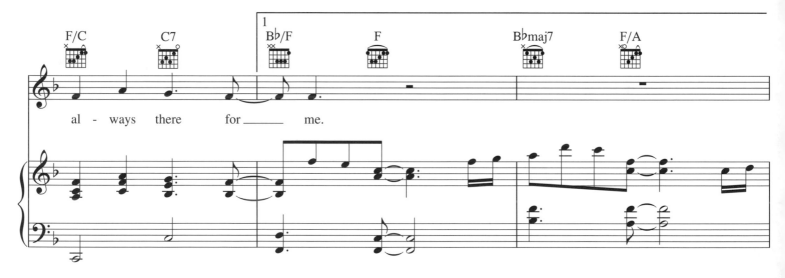

al - ways there for _____ me.

When life _____ me.

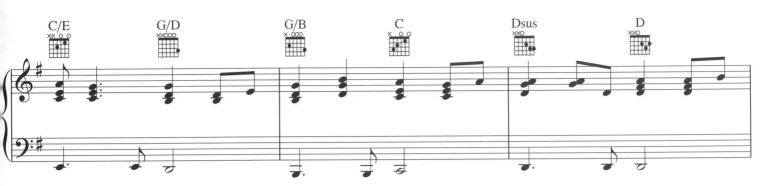

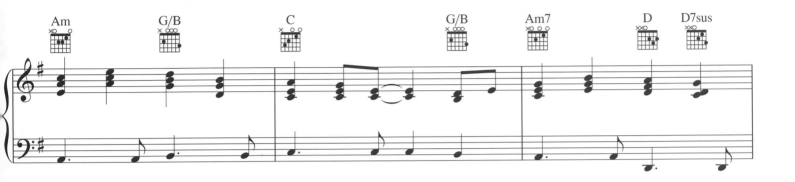

You are there when I most need you, you are

there so con - stant - ly. _____ And you come shin - ing through, you

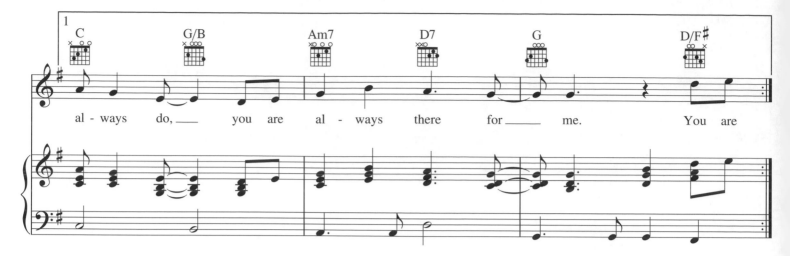

al - ways do, ___ you are al - ways there for ___ me. You are

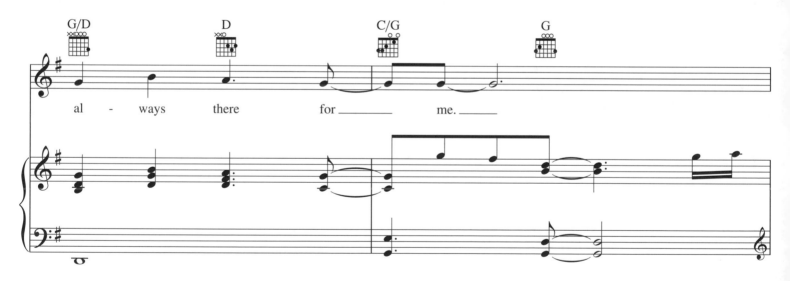

al - ways do, _____ you are

al - ways there for ___ me. ___

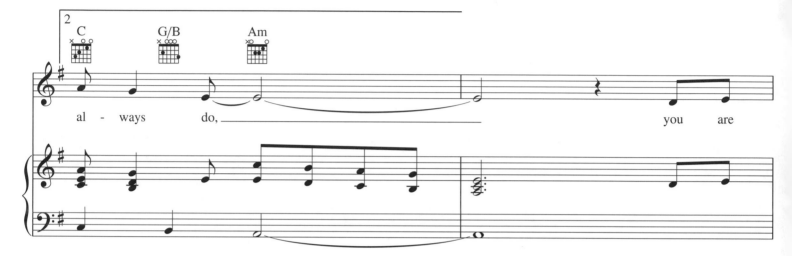

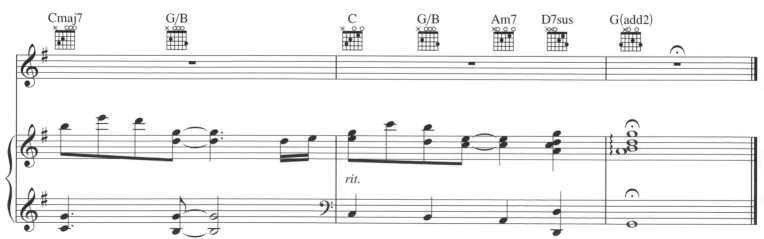

rit.

ANGELS

Words and Music by AMY GRANT,
GARY CHAPMAN, MICHAEL W. SMITH
and BROWN BANNISTER

"Take this man to pris - on," the man___ heard Her - od say,___ and
on - ly knows the times___ my life was threat - ened just to - day.___ A

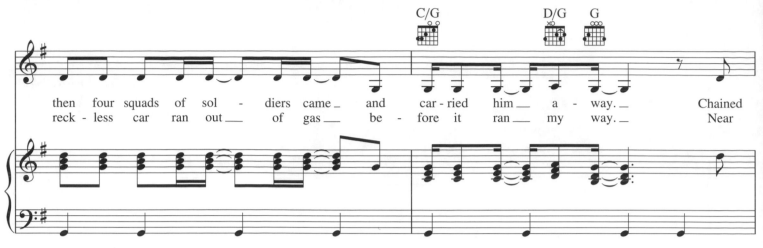

then four squads of sol - diers came __ and car - ried him __ a - way. __ Chained
reck - less car ran out __ of gas __ be - fore it ran __ my way. __ Near

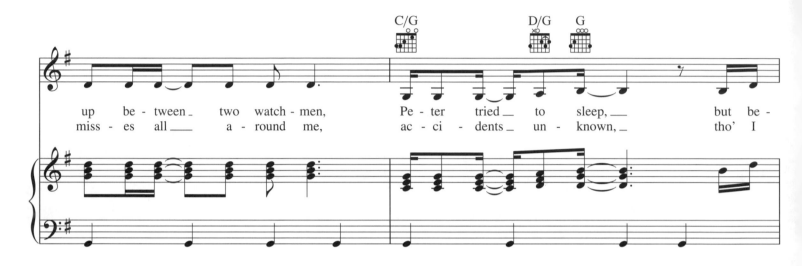

up be - tween __ two watch - men, Pe - ter tried __ to sleep, __ but be -
miss - es all __ a - round me, ac - ci - dents __ un - known, __ tho' I

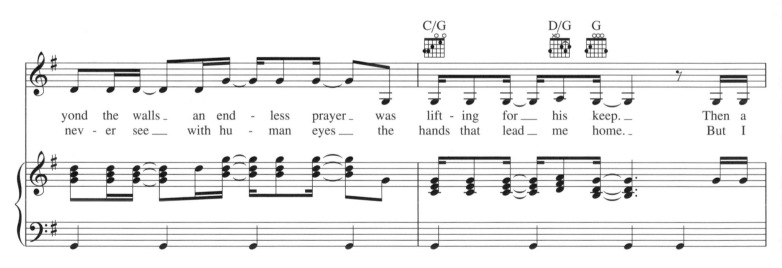

yond the walls __ an end - less prayer __ was lift - ing for __ his keep. __ Then a
nev - er see __ with hu - man eyes __ the hands that lead __ me home. __ But I

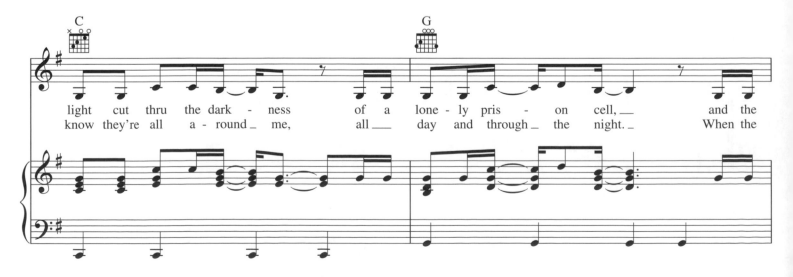

light cut thru the dark - ness of a lone - ly pris - on cell, __ and the
know they're all a - round me, all __ day and through __ the night. __ When the

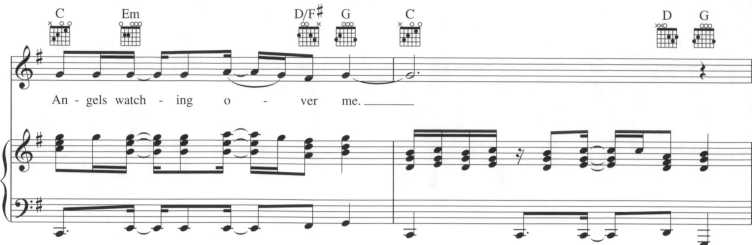

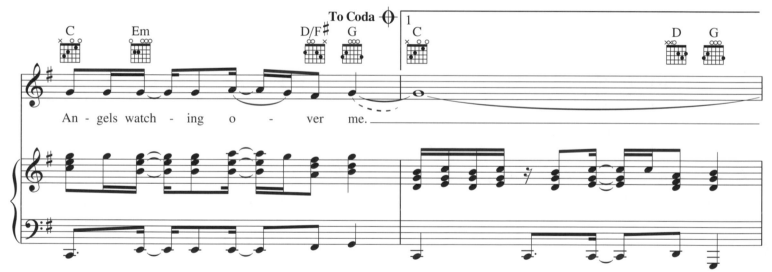

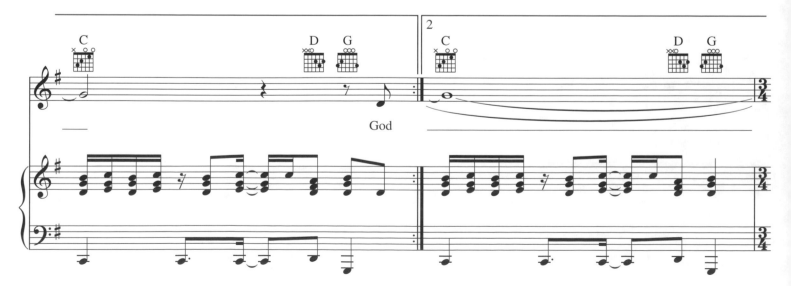

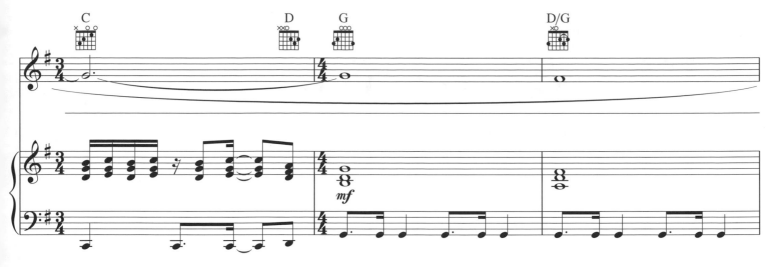

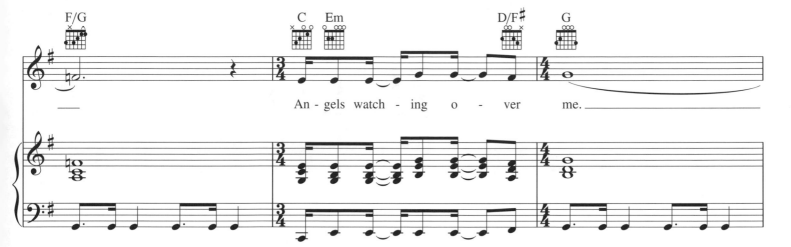

An - gels watch - ing o - ver me.

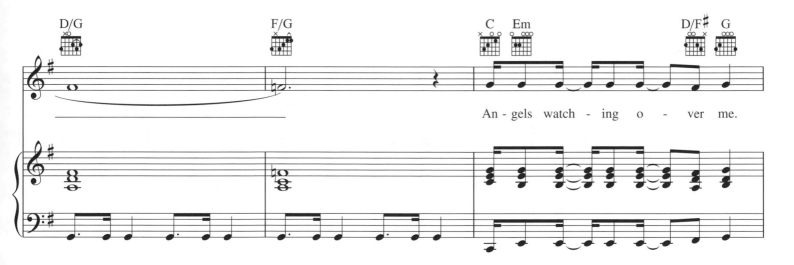

An - gels watch - ing o - ver me.

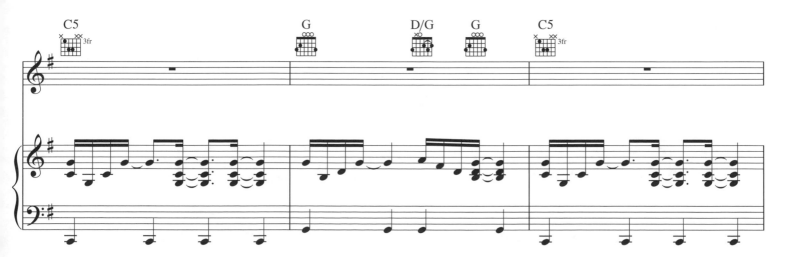

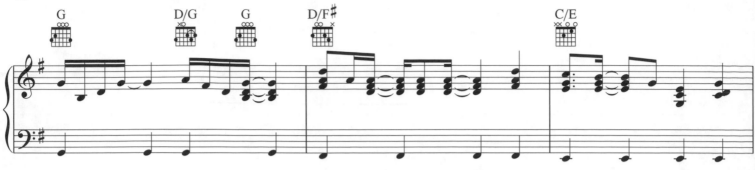

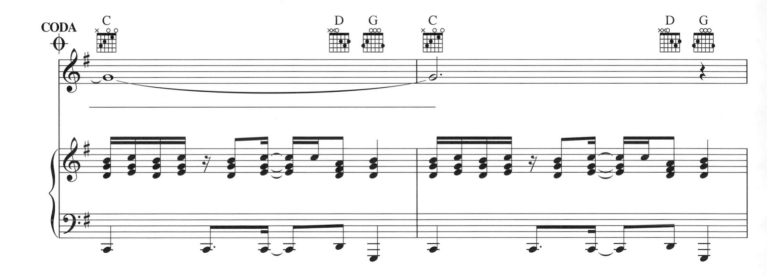

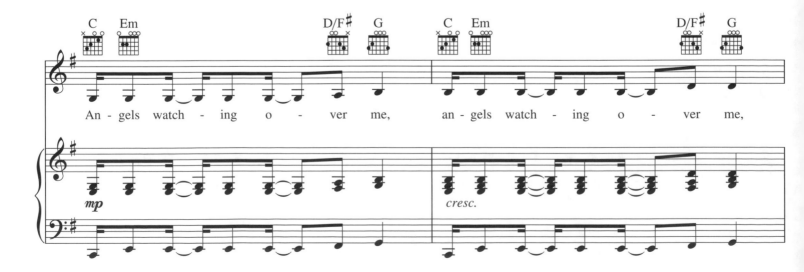

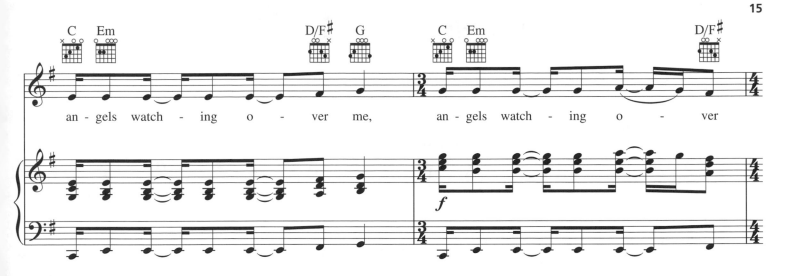

an - gels watch - ing o - ver me, an - gels watch - ing o - ver

me. _____ Tho' I nev - er see ___ with hu - man eyes ___ the hands ___

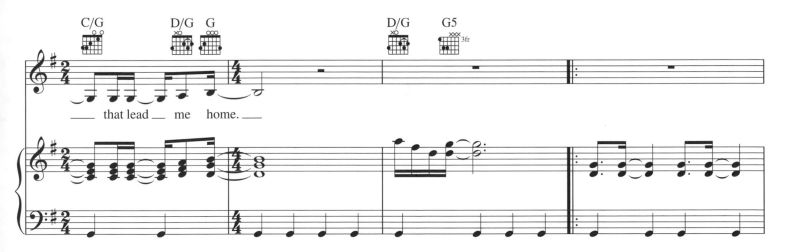

___ that lead ___ me home. ___

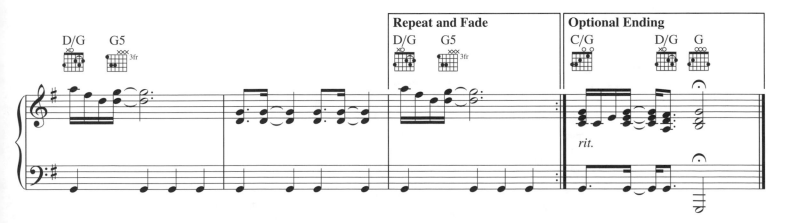

ARISE, MY LOVE

Words and Music by
EDDIE CARSWELL

Slowly, mysteriously

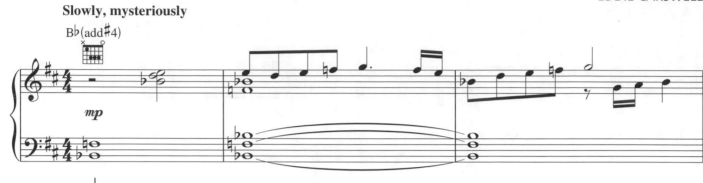

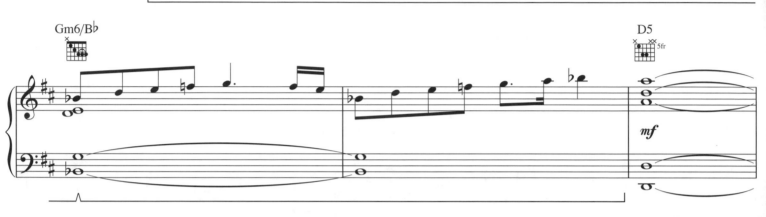

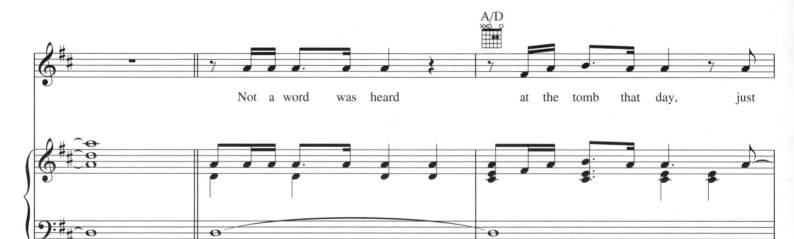

Not a word was heard at the tomb that day, just

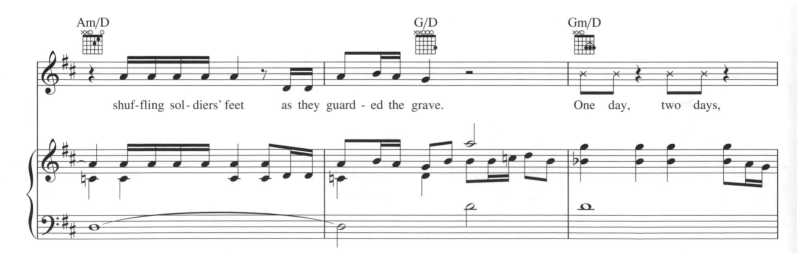

shuf-fling sol-diers' feet as they guard-ed the grave. One day, two days,

my Love, ___ a - rise, ___ my Love. __ The grave __ no __ long - er has a hold __

_____ on __ You. No more _____ death's sting, no more suf - fer - ing. A -

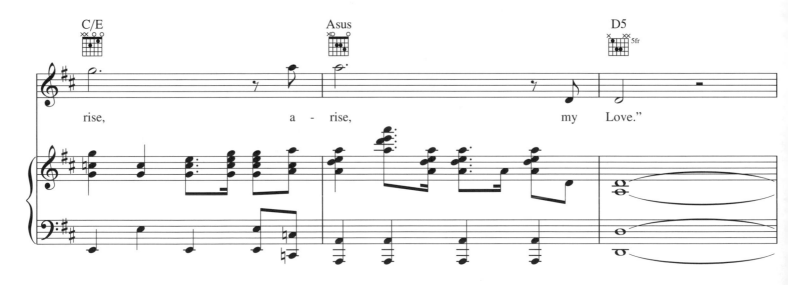

rise, a - rise, my Love."

The earth trem - bled and the tomb be - gan to shake,

and like light-ning from heav-en the stone rolled _ a - way. And as dead men, the guards

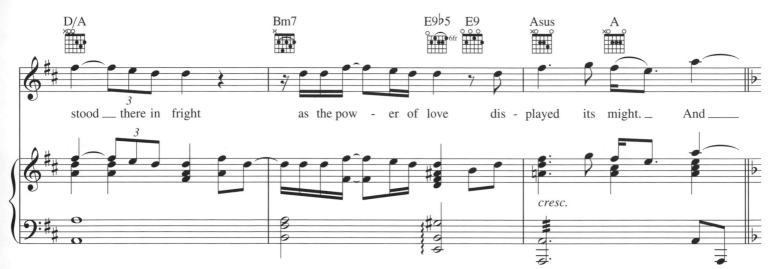

stood _ there in fright as the pow - er of love dis - played its might. _ And _

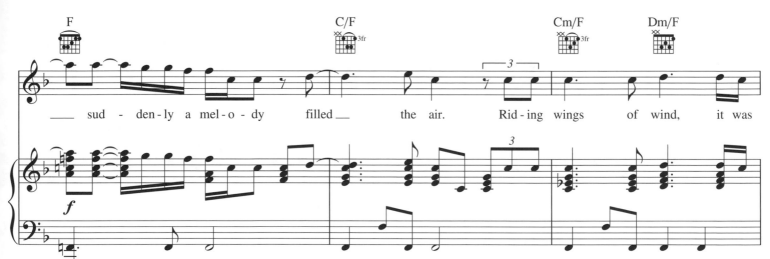

_ sud - den-ly a mel-o-dy filled _ the air. Rid - ing wings of wind, it was

ev - 'ry - where. _ The words all cre-a-tion had been long - ing to hear, _ a

sweet __ sound of vic- t'ry, so __ loud and __ clear: _____ "A - rise, __

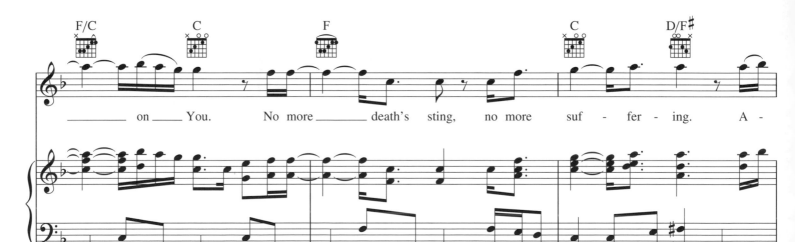

_____ my Love, __ a - rise, __ my Love. __ The grave __ no __ long- er has a hold __

_____ on __ You. No more _____ death's sting, no more suf - fer - ing. A -

rise, a - rise."

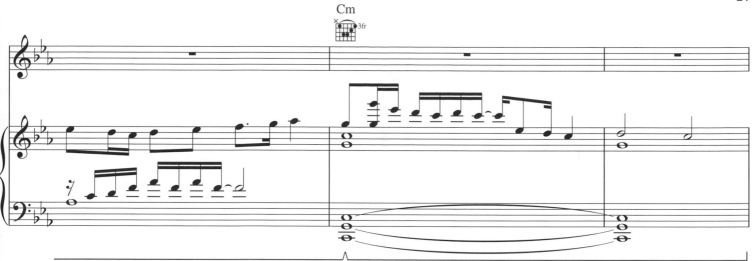

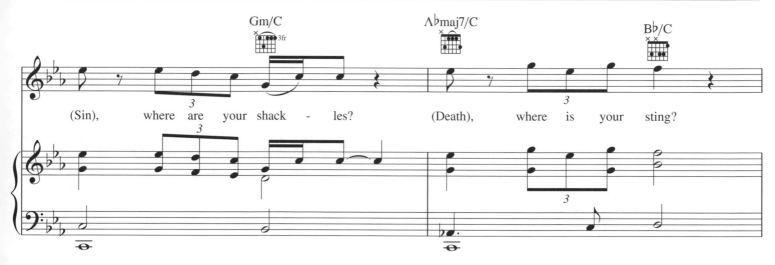

(Sin), where are your shack - les? (Death), where is your sting?

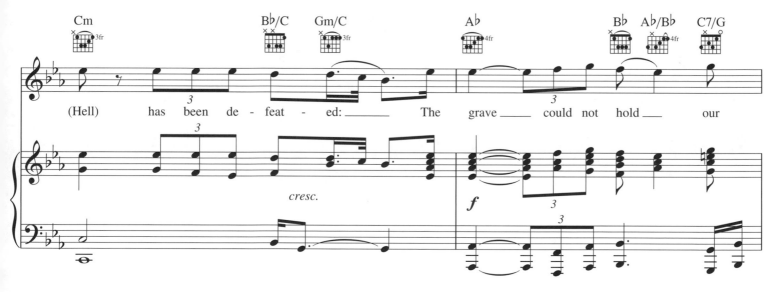

(Hell) has been de - feat - ed: _____ The grave _____ could not hold _____ our

cresc.

f

King.

"A - rise, __

my Love, ___ a - rise, ___ my Love. _ The grave _

__ no _ long - er has a hold ____ on _ You. No more ___ death's sting, no more

suf - fer - ing. A - rise, ____ a - rise, ____ a -

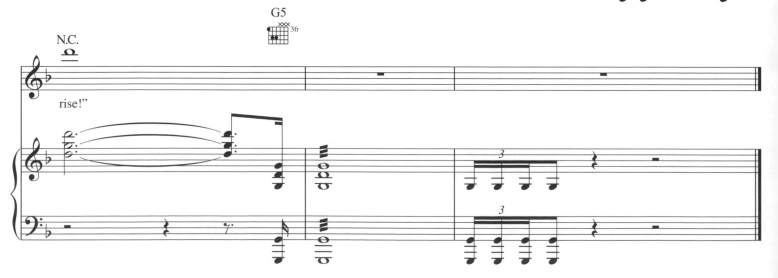

rise!"

CAN'T LIVE A DAY

Words and Music by TY LACY,
CONNIE HARRINGTON and JOE BECK

of what could be ___ with ev - 'ry star ___ so far ___ and out ___ of reach.
be - yond ___ com - pare, ___ to grant my ev - 'ry wish ___ with - out ___ a care.

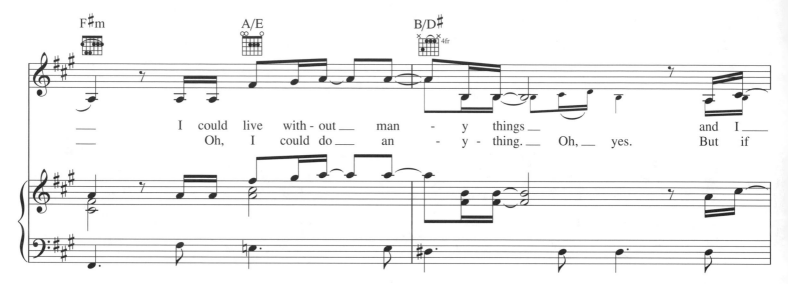

___ I could live with - out ___ man - y things ___ and I ___
___ Oh, I could do ___ an - y - thing. ___ Oh, ___ yes. But if

___ could car - ry on. ___ But I
You weren't in ___ it all, ___ I } could - n't face ___ my life ___ to - mor - row with - out Your hope ___

___ in my ___ heart. I ___ know ___ I can't live a day ___ with - out ___ You. ___

(Harmony 2nd time only)

Lord, there's __ no night __ and there's __ no morn - ing with - out Your lov -

- ing arms __ to hold __ me. _____ You're the heart - beat of all _____ I do. __

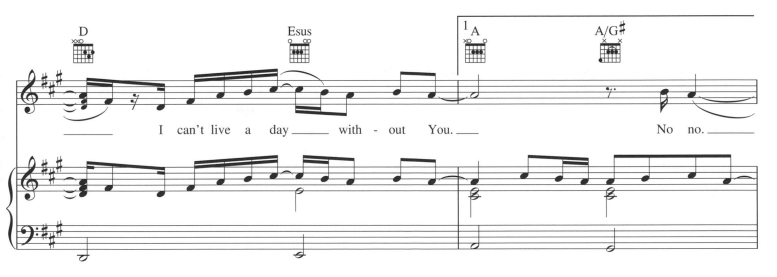

_____ I can't live a day _____ with - out You. ___ No no. _____

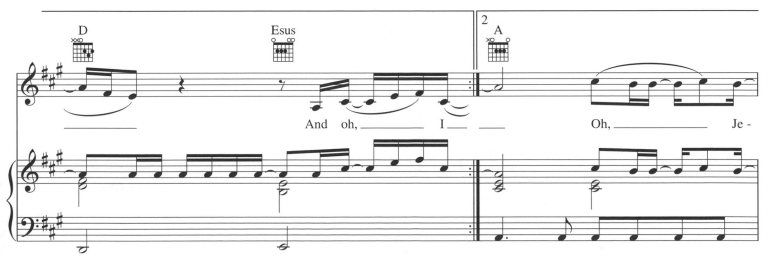

And oh, _____ I ___ Oh, _____ Je -

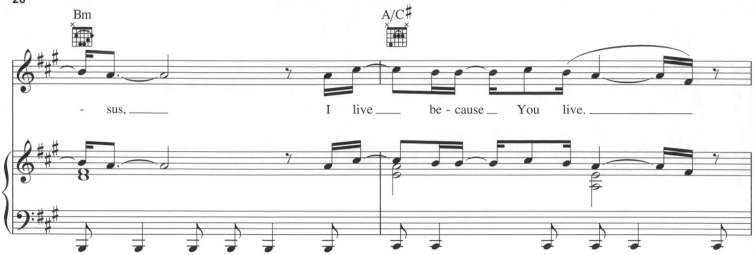

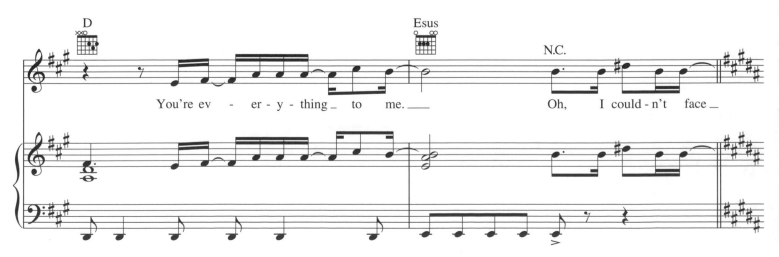

Oh. _____

_____ my life _____ to - mor - row with - out Your hope _____ in my _____ heart. I _____ know _____ I

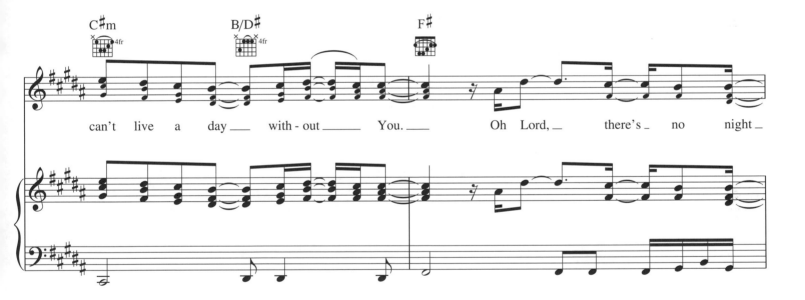

can't live a day _____ with - out _____ You. _____ Oh Lord, _____ there's _____ no night _____

_____ and there's _____ no morn - ing with - out Your lov - ing arms _____ to hold _____ me. _____ You're the

I can't live a day _____ with - out _____ You. _____

heart - beat of all _____ I do. _____ I could - n't face _

_____ my life _ to - mor - row with - out Your hope _____ in my _ heart. I _____ know, _

I know. _____

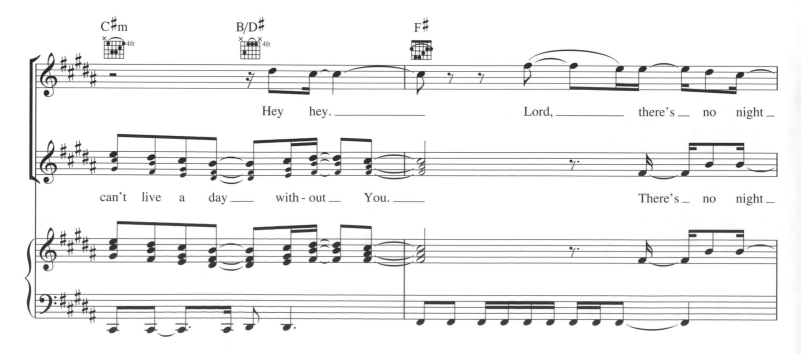

Hey hey. _____ Lord, _____ there's _ no night _

can't live a day _____ with - out _ You. _____ There's _ no night _

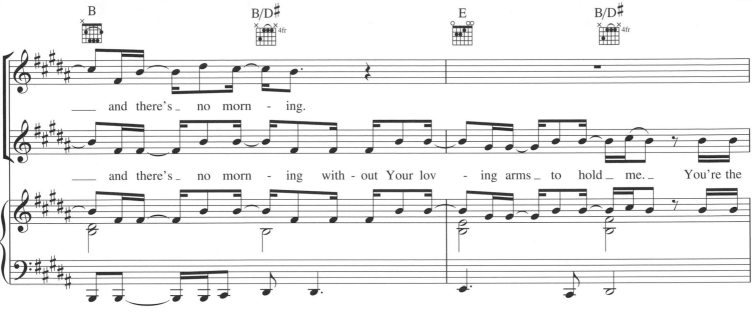

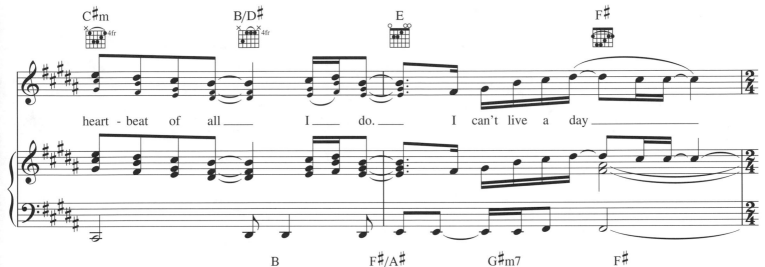

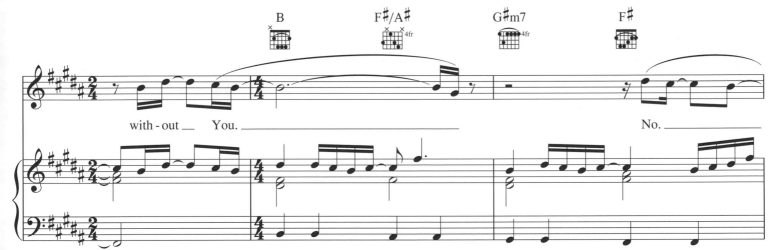

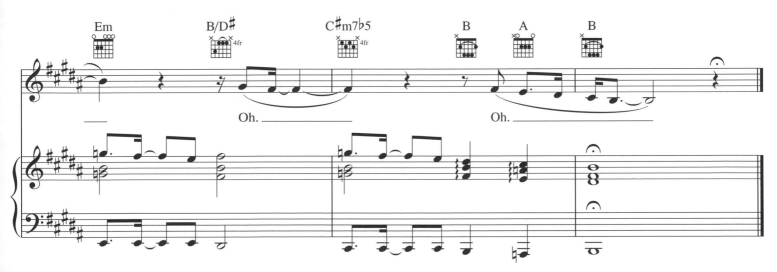

EVERY HEART THAT IS BREAKING

Words and Music by
TWILA PARIS

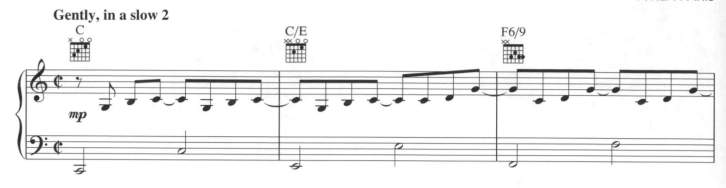

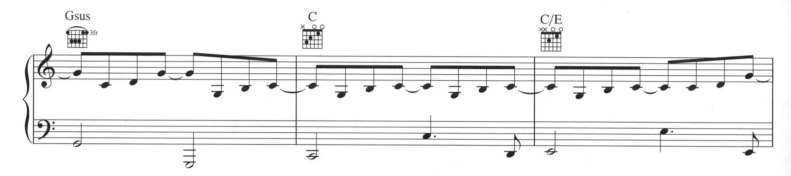

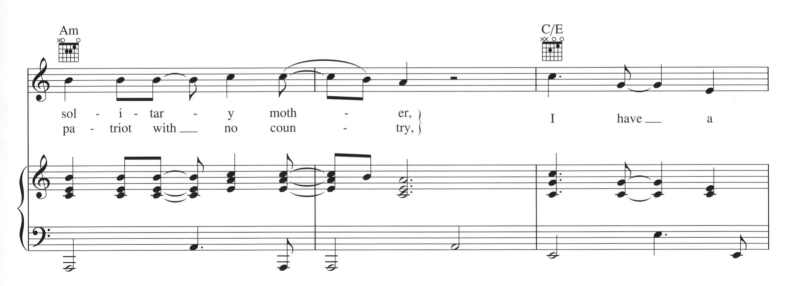

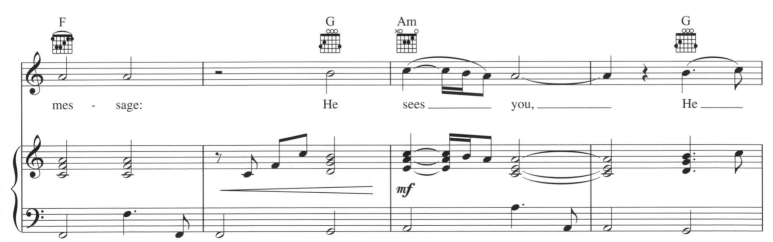

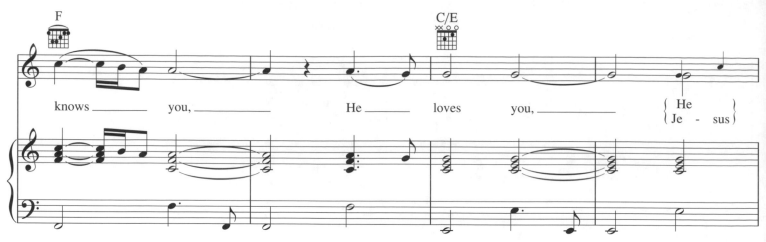

knows _____ you, _____ He _____ loves you, _____ { He }
{ Je - sus }

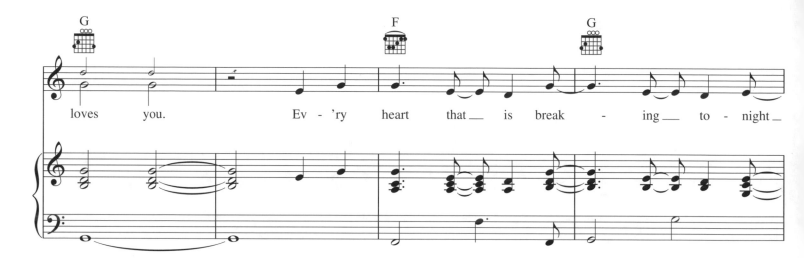

loves you. Ev - 'ry heart that __ is break - ing __ to - night __

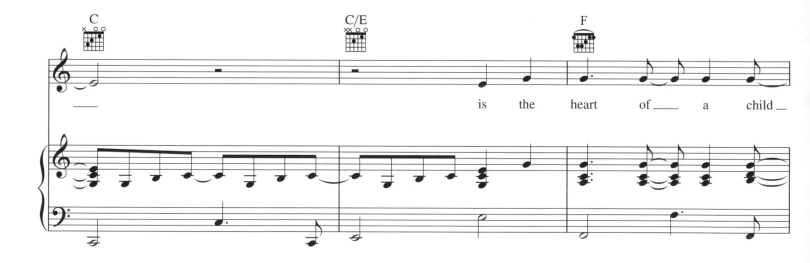

____ is the heart of ___ a child __

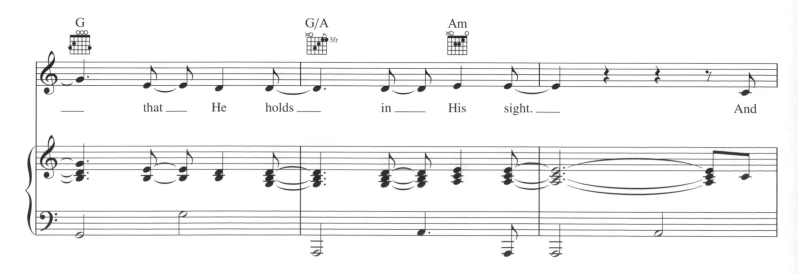

____ that ___ He holds ___ in ___ His sight. ___ And

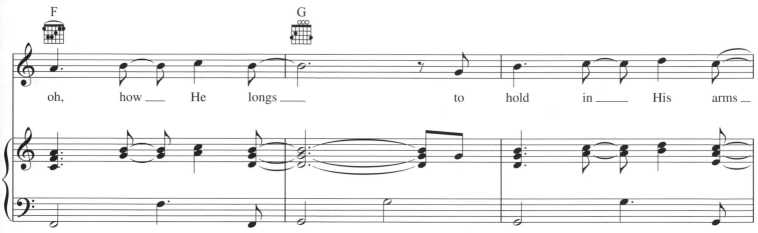

oh, how ___ He longs ___ to hold in ___ His arms ___

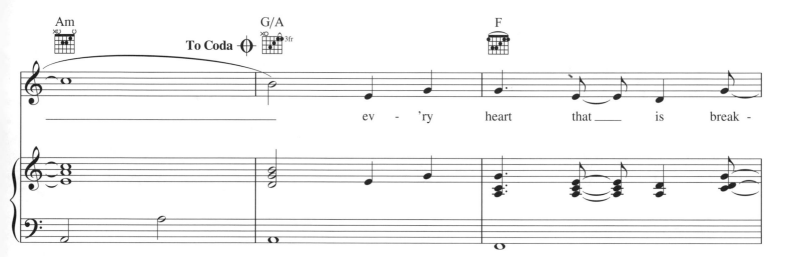

___ ev - 'ry heart that ___ is break -

- ing ___ to - night, ___ ev - 'ry

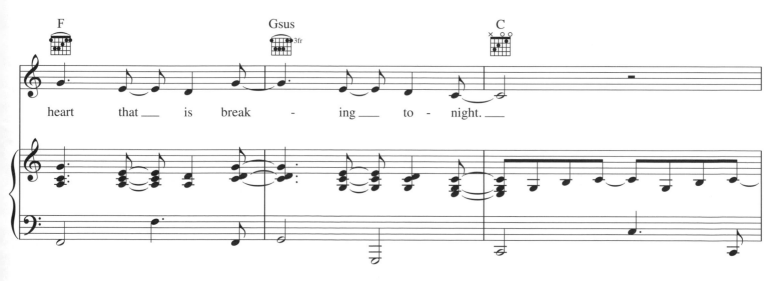

heart that ___ is break - ing ___ to - night. ___

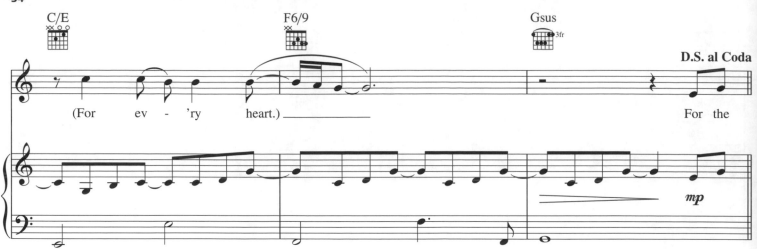

(For ev - 'ry heart.) _____ For the

D.S. al Coda

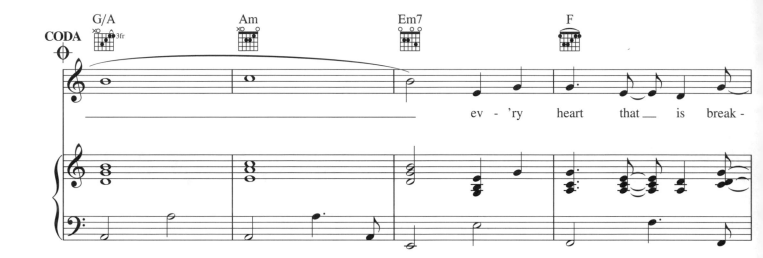

CODA

ev - 'ry heart that __ is break-

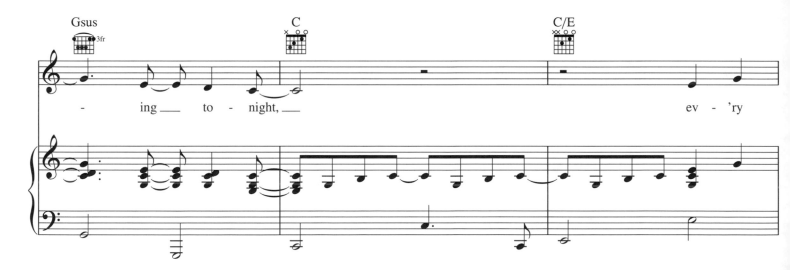

- ing __ to - night, __ ev - 'ry

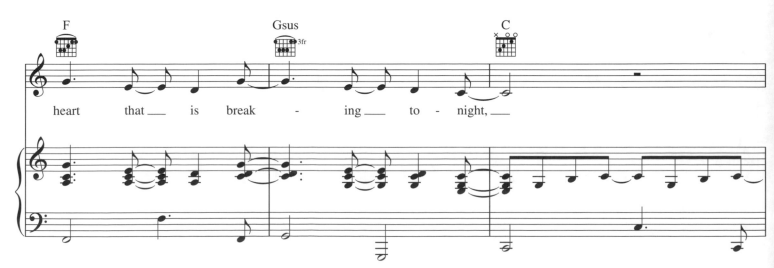

heart that __ is break - ing __ to - night, __

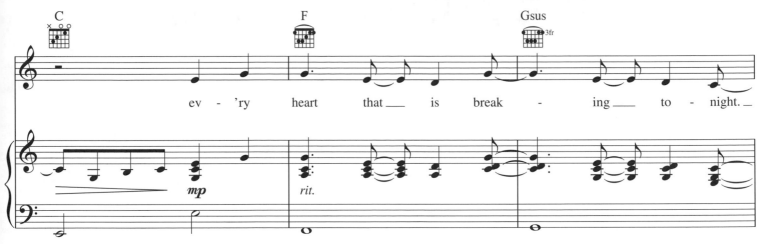

ev - 'ry heart that ___ is break - ing ___ to - night. ___

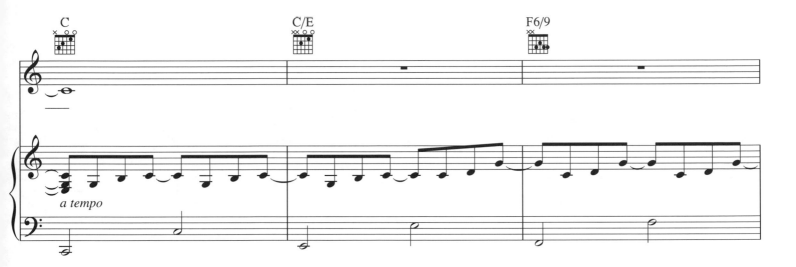

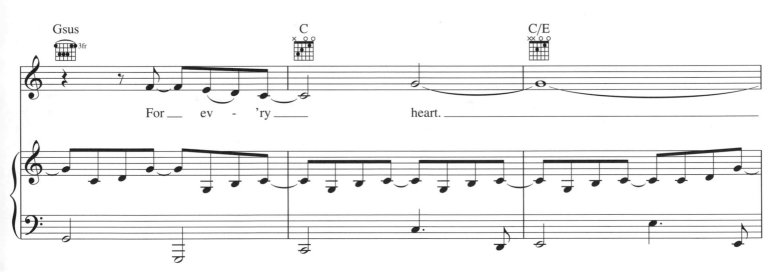

For ___ ev - 'ry ___ heart. ___

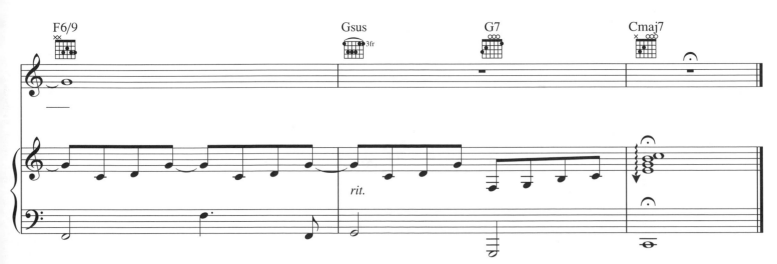

GOD AND GOD ALONE

Words and Music by
PHILL McHUGH

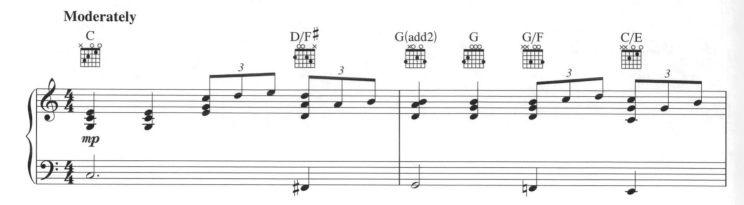

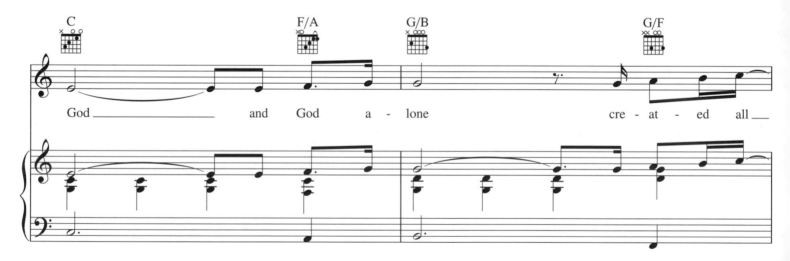

God _____ and God a - lone cre - at - ed all __

___ these things we call our own. From the

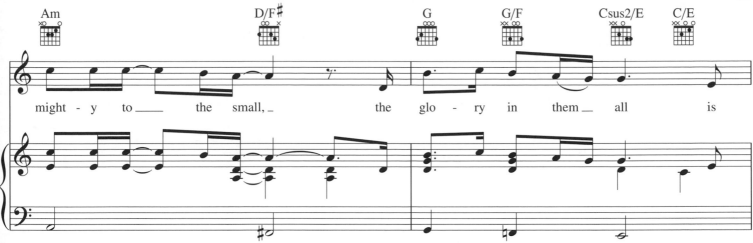

might-y to ____ the small, __ the glo-ry in them __ all ____ is

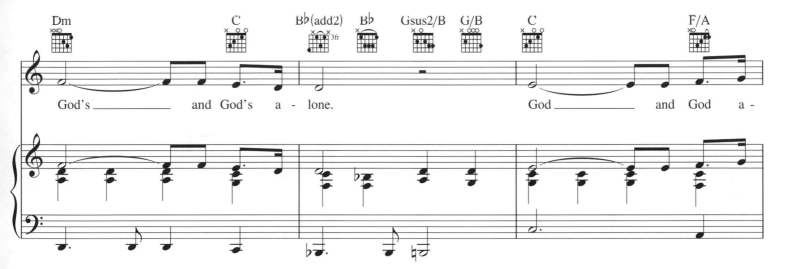

God's _____ and God's a - lone. ____ God _____ and God a-

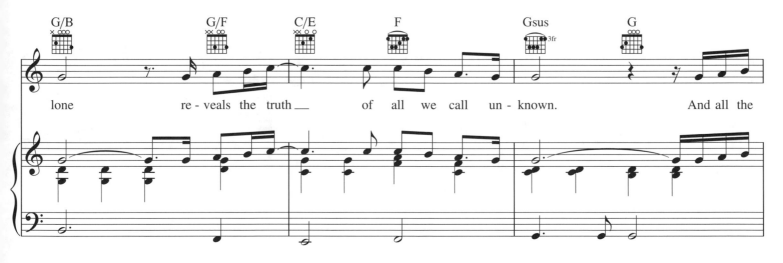

lone ____ re-veals the truth __ of all we call un-known. ____ And all the

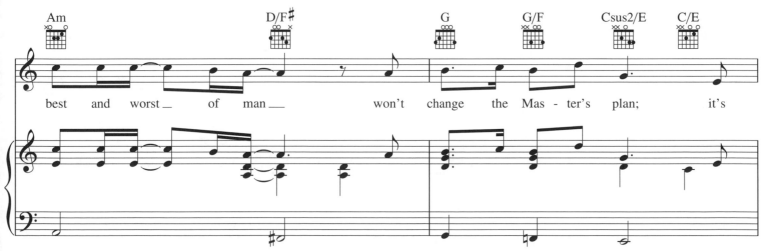

best and worst __ of man __ won't change the Mas-ter's plan; __ it's

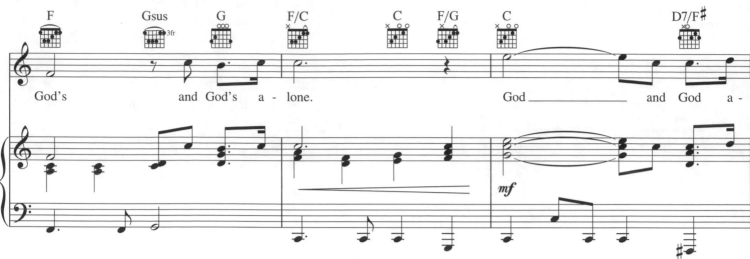

God's and God's a - lone. God and God a -

lone is fit to take the u - ni - verse - 's throne.

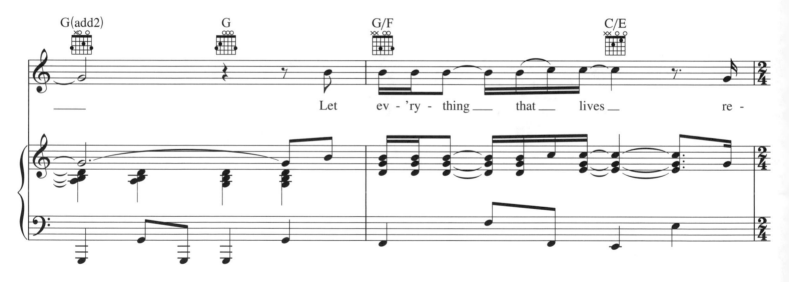

Let ev - 'ry - thing that lives re -

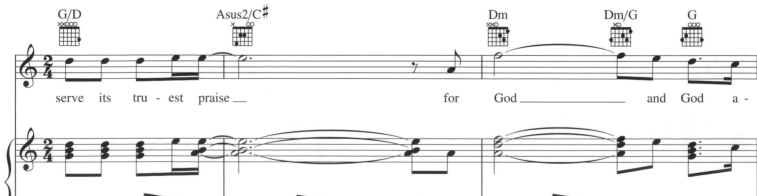

serve its tru - est praise for God and God a -

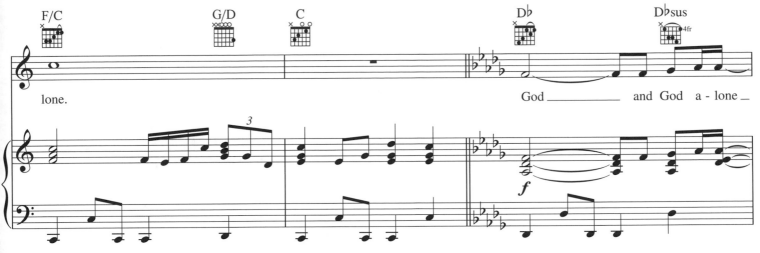

lone.

God _____ and God a - lone _

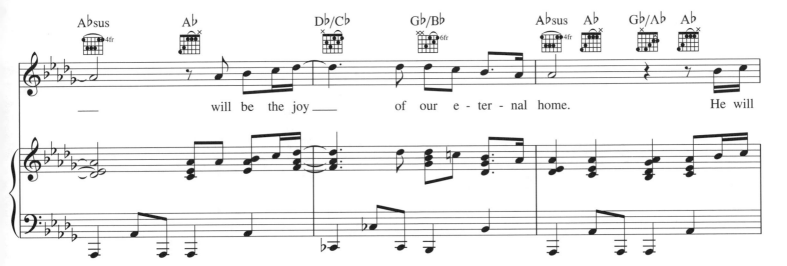

_____ will be the joy ____ of our e - ter - nal home. He will

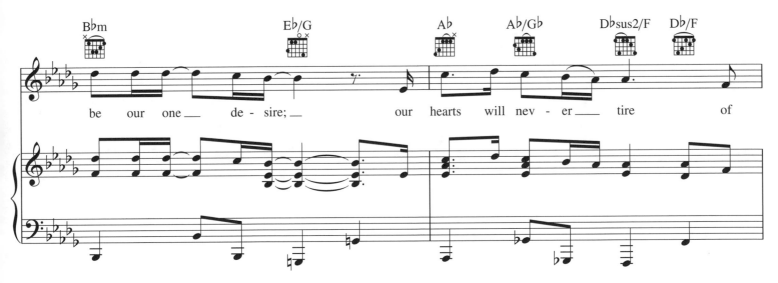

be our one ____ de - sire; ___ our hearts will nev - er ___ tire of

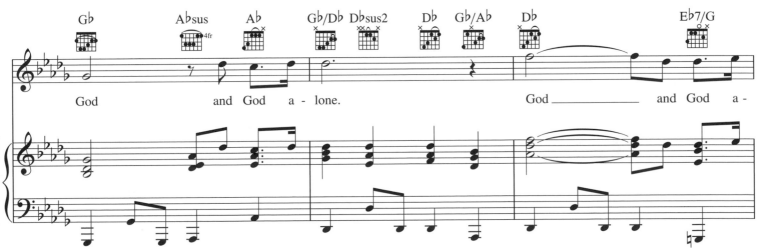

God and God a - lone.

God _____ and God a -

lone   is   fit   to   take ___   the   u - ni - verse - 's   throne. ___

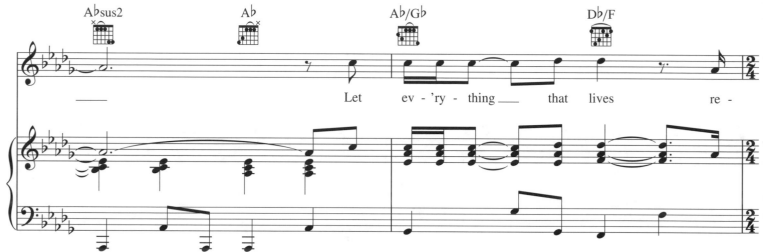

___   Let   ev - 'ry - thing ___   that   lives   re -

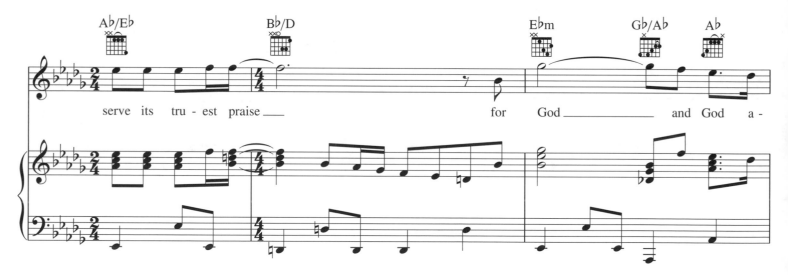

serve   its   tru - est   praise ___   for   God _____   and   God   a -

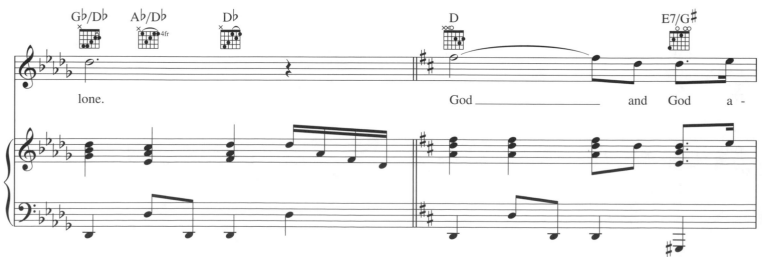

lone.   God _____   and   God   a -

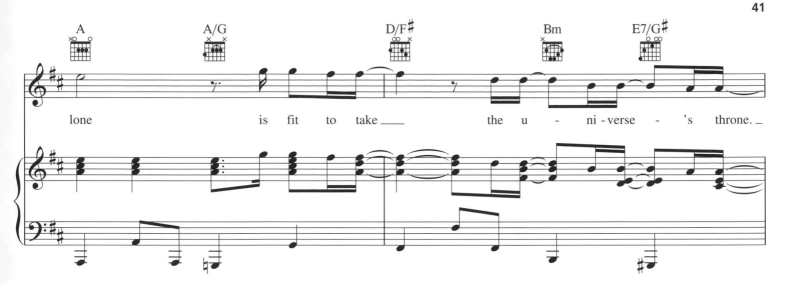

lone _____ is fit to take _____ the u - ni - verse - 's throne. _____

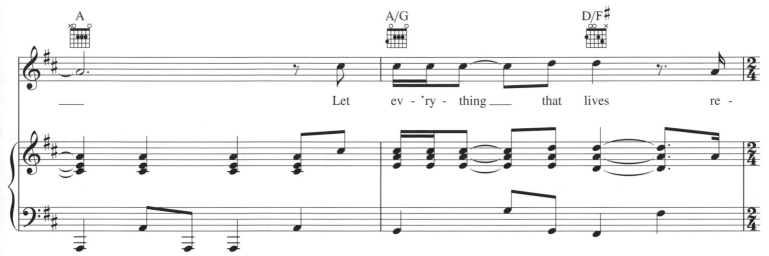

_____ Let ev - 'ry - thing _____ that lives re -

serve its tru - est praise _____ for God and

God... Let ev - 'ry - thing _____ that _____ lives _____ re -

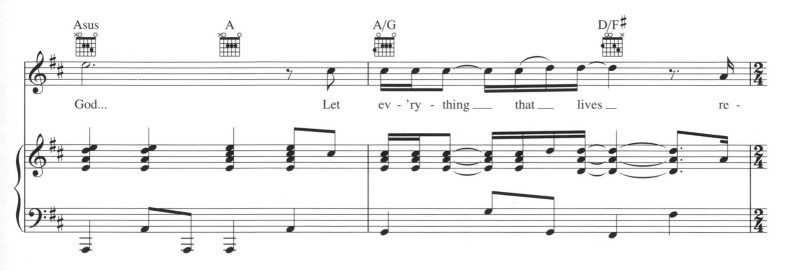

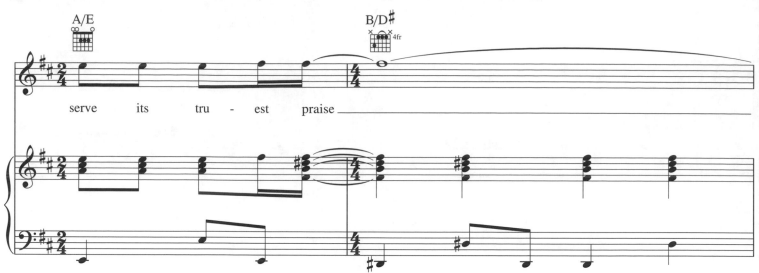

serve its tru - est praise _____

_____ for God and God a -

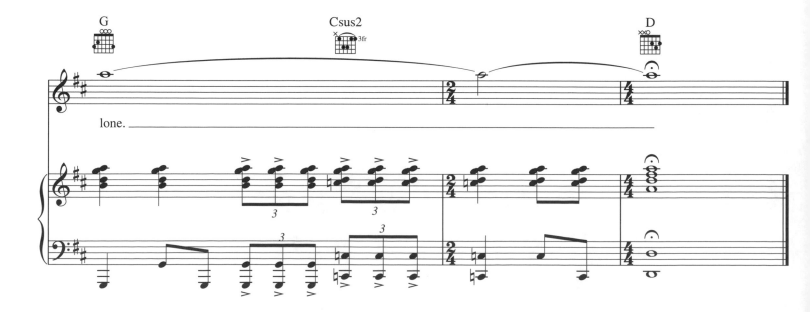

lone. _____

HEALING HANDS

Words and Music by GRANT CUNNINGHAM,
MATT HUESMANN and JONATHAN PIERCE

With feeling

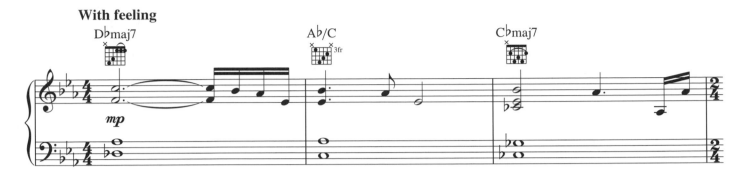

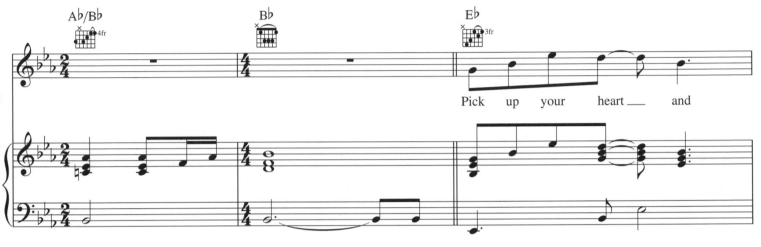

Pick up your heart ___ and

car-ry it to ___ heal-ing hands. ___

There is no scar, ___ no pain He won't un-der-stand. ___

Those bro - ken dreams ___ you've car - ried this far ___

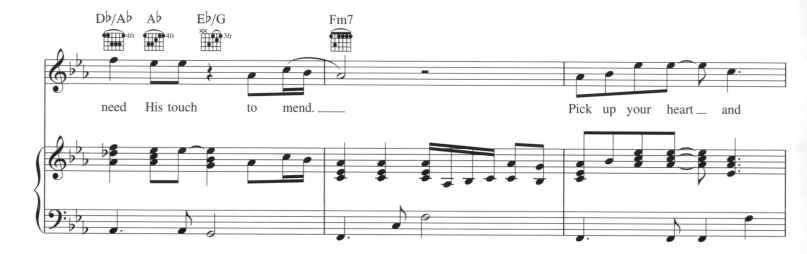

need His touch to mend. ___ Pick up your heart ___ and

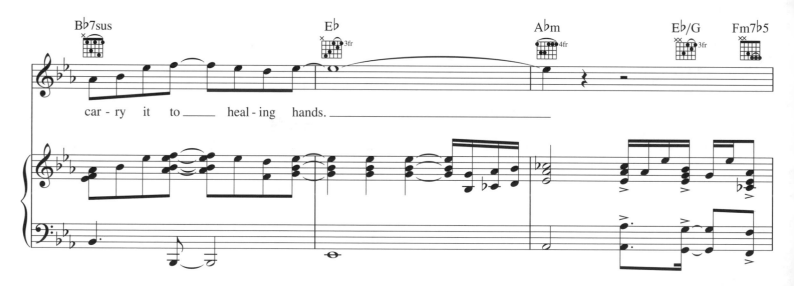

car - ry it to ___ heal - ing hands. ___

What brought you here ___ to this time, to the place ___ where your own ___

strength has found its end, _____ and the

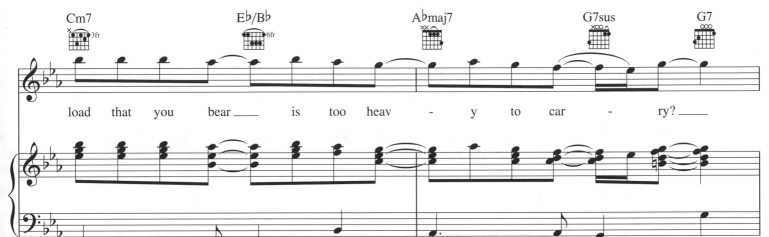

load that you bear ____ is too heav - y to car - ry? ____

Come, bring it all ____ to ____ Him. ____ Pick up your heart ___ and

car - ry it to ____ heal - ing hands. ____

He won't un - der - stand. ___ Those

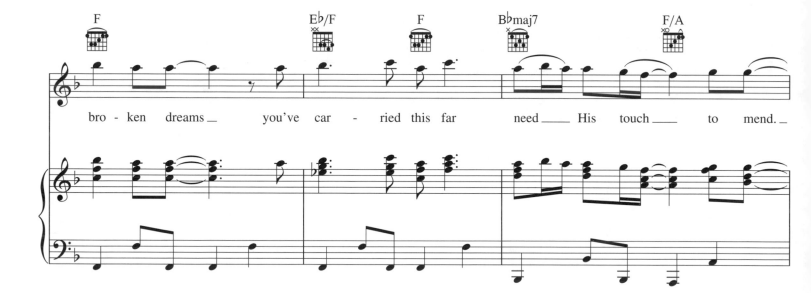

bro - ken dreams ___ you've car - ried this far ___ need ___ His touch ___ to mend. __

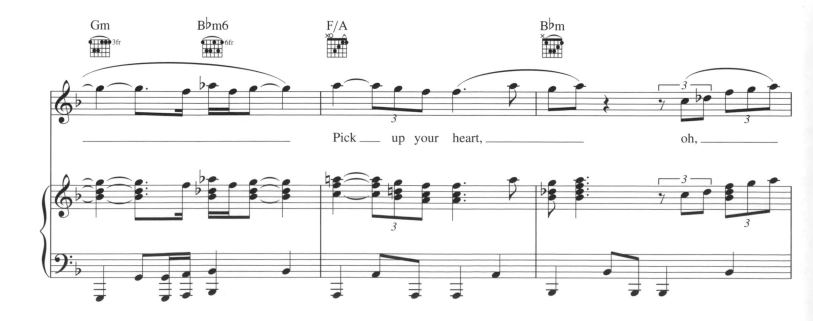

Pick ___ up your heart, _____ oh, _____

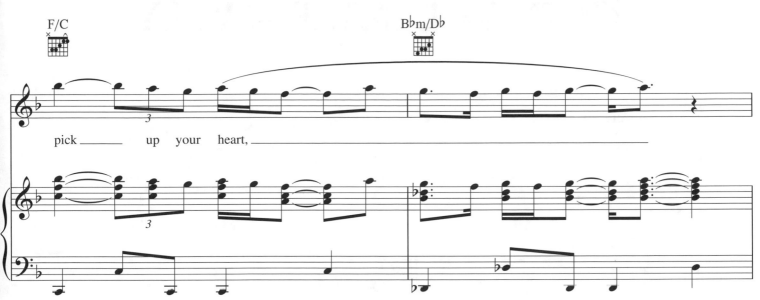

pick _____ up your heart, _____ _____

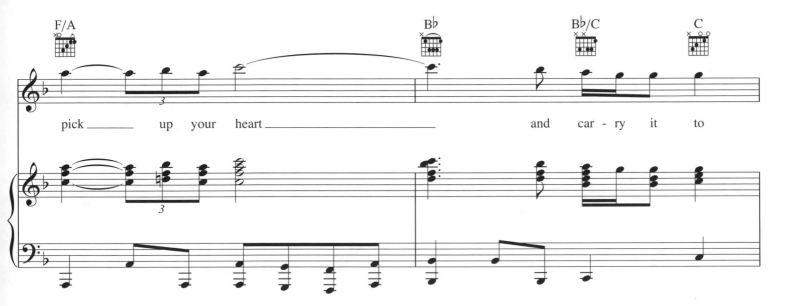

pick _____ up your heart _____ and car - ry it to

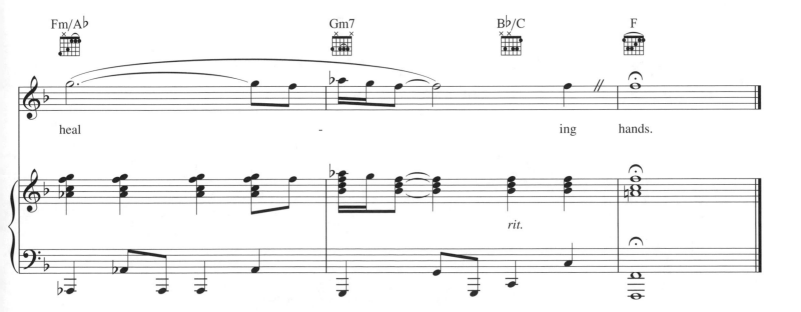

heal - ing hands.

rit.

GOD WILL MAKE A WAY

Words and Music by
DON MOEN

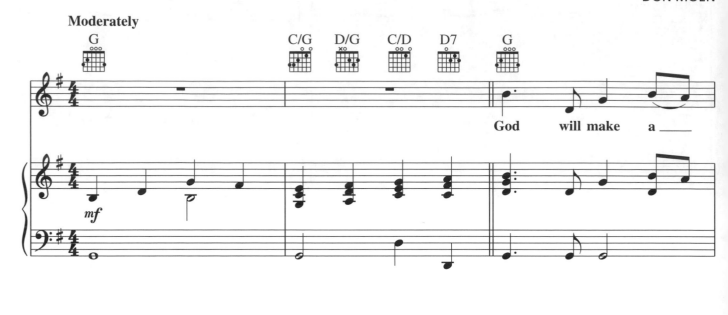

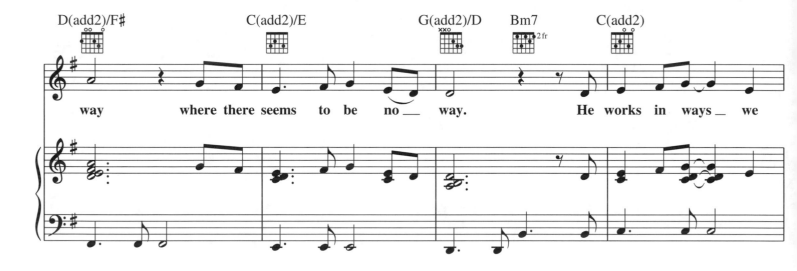

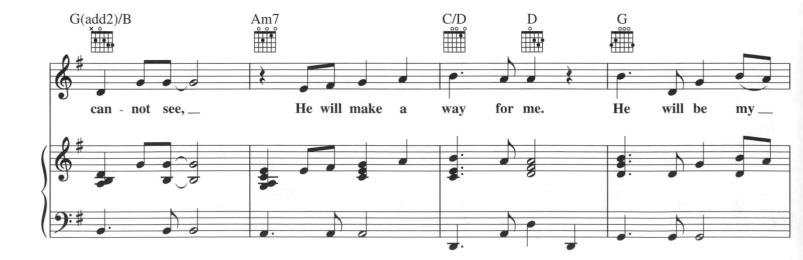

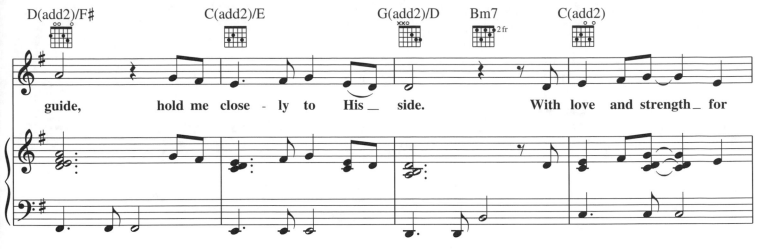

guide, hold me close - ly to His __ side. With love and strength __ for

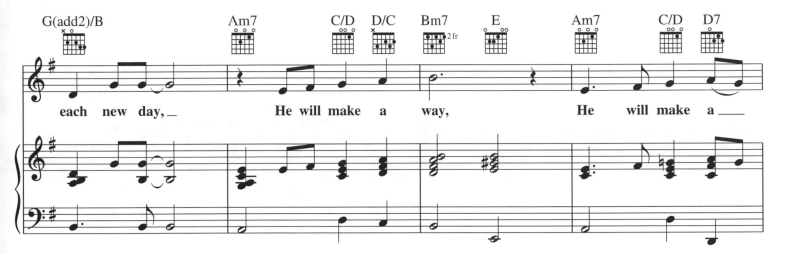

each new day, __ He will make a way, He will make a ____

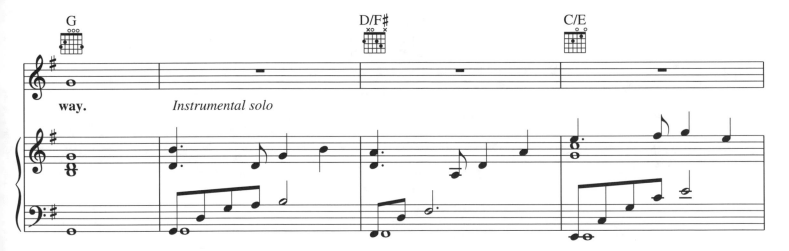

way. *Instrumental solo*

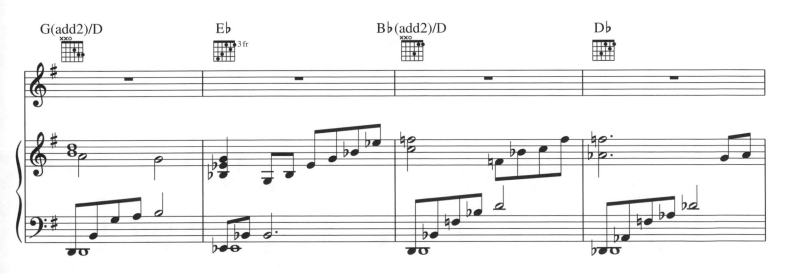

Solo ends   By a

road - way   in   the   wil - der - ness __   He'll   lead ____   me.

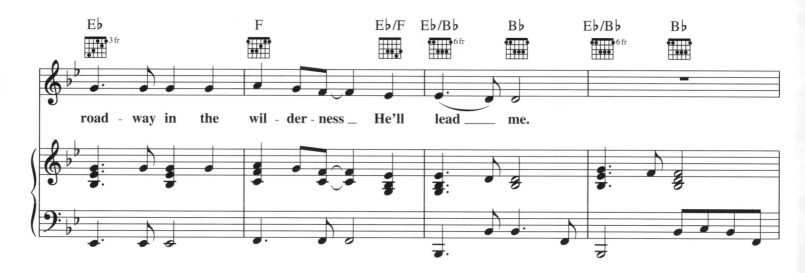

Riv - ers   in   the   des - ert   will __   I   see.

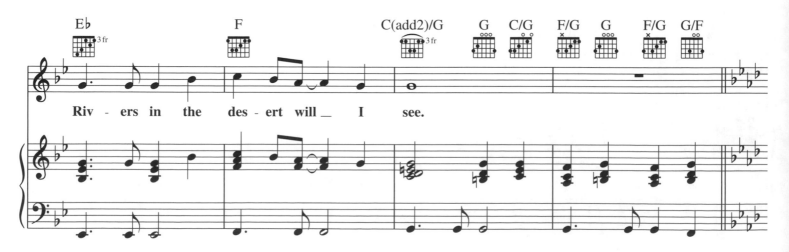

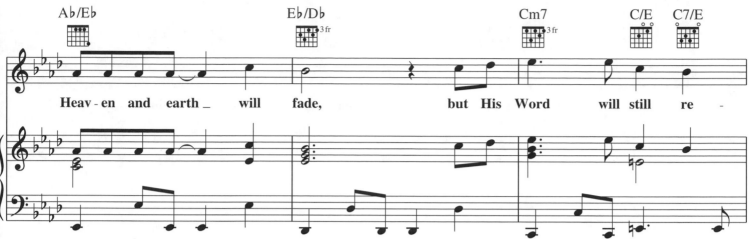

Heav-en and earth __ will fade, but His Word will still re-

main. He will do __ some-thing new __ to-day. __

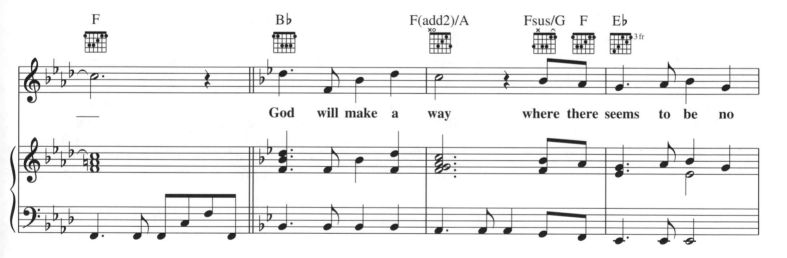

__ God will make a way where there seems to be no

way. He works in ways __ we can-not see, __ He will make a

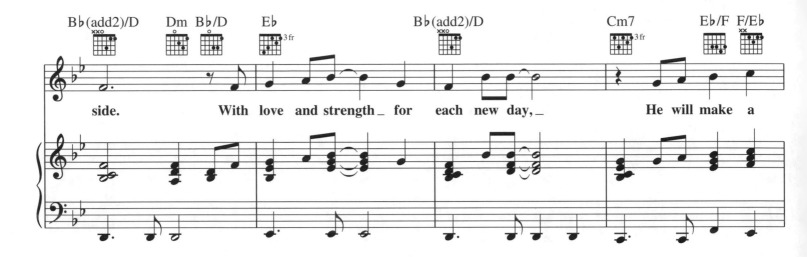

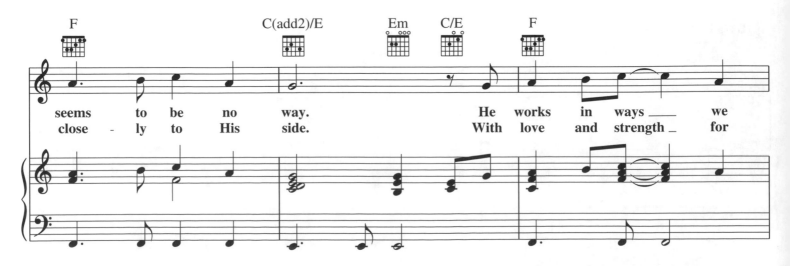

GRACE BY WHICH I STAND

Words and Music by
KEITH GREEN

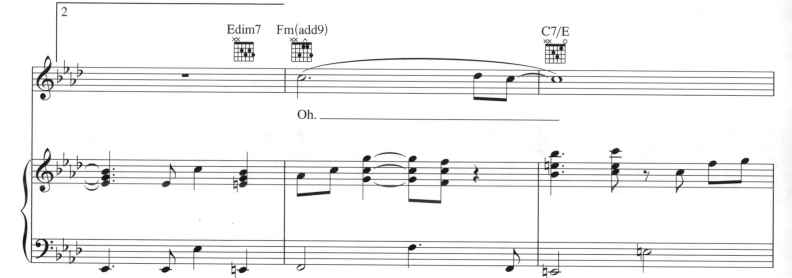

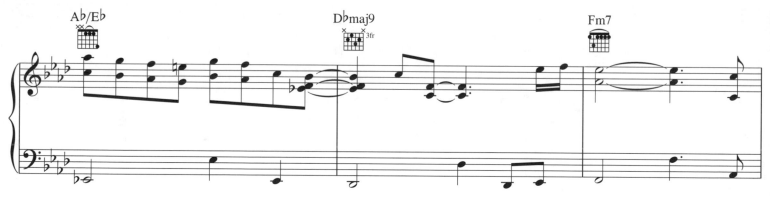

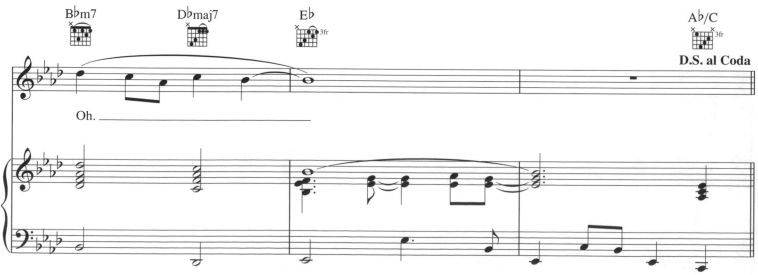

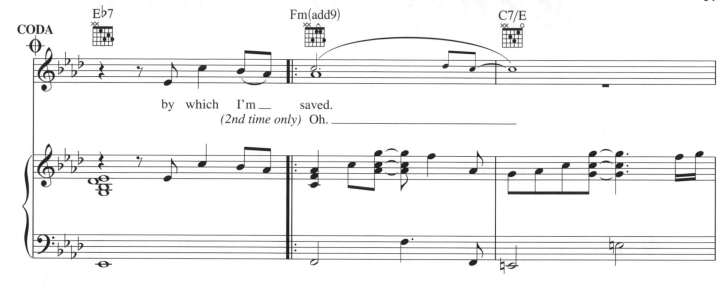

by which I'm___ saved.
(2nd time only) Oh. _____

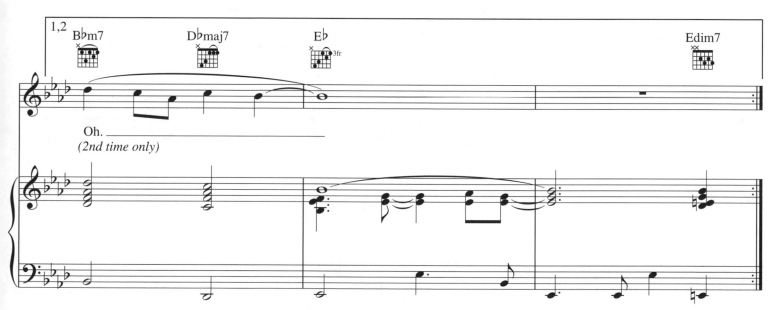

Oh. _____
(2nd time only)

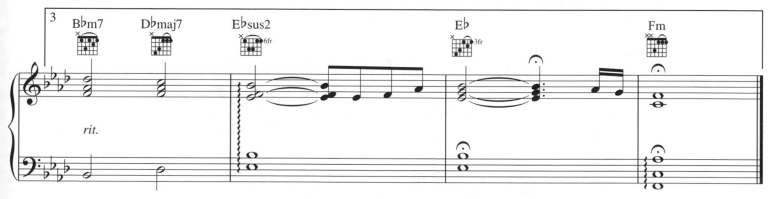

rit.

HIS STRENGTH IS PERFECT

Words and Music by STEVEN CURTIS CHAPMAN
and JERRY SALLEY

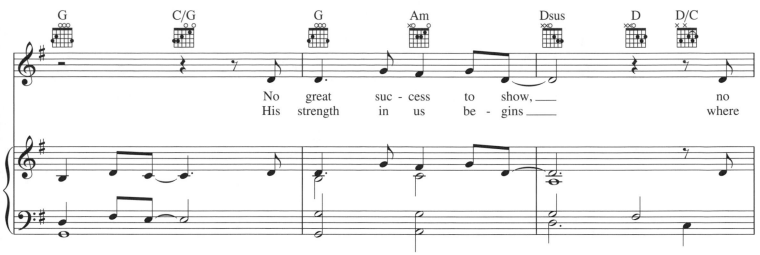

No great suc-cess to show, ___ no
His strength in us be - gins ___ where

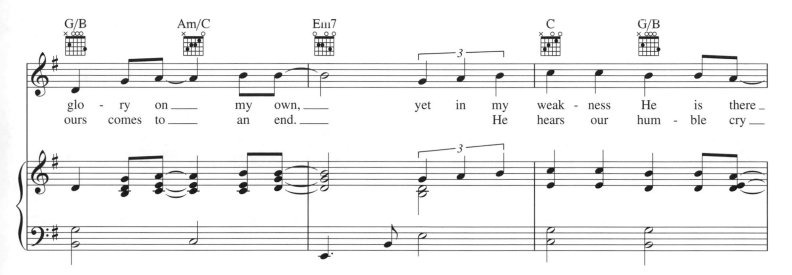

glo - ry on ___ my own, ___ yet in my weak - ness He is there ___
ours comes to ___ an end. ___ He hears our hum - ble cry ___

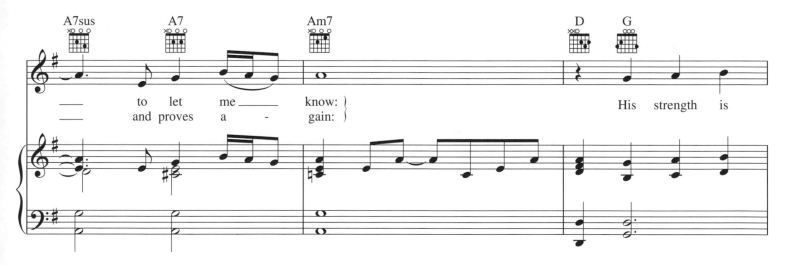

___ to let me ___ know: } His strength is
___ and proves a - gain: }

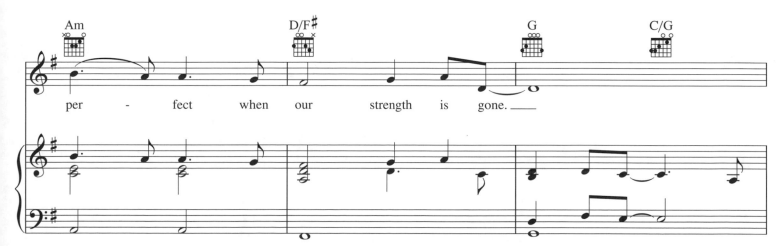

per - fect when our strength is gone. ___

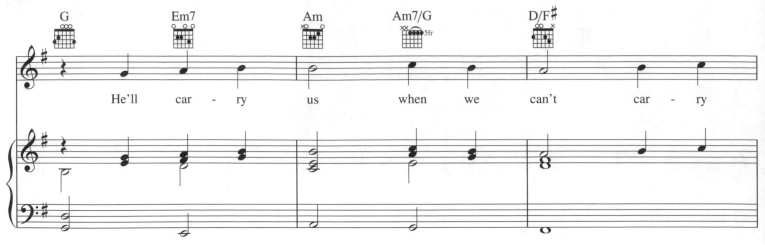

He'll car - ry us when we can't car - ry

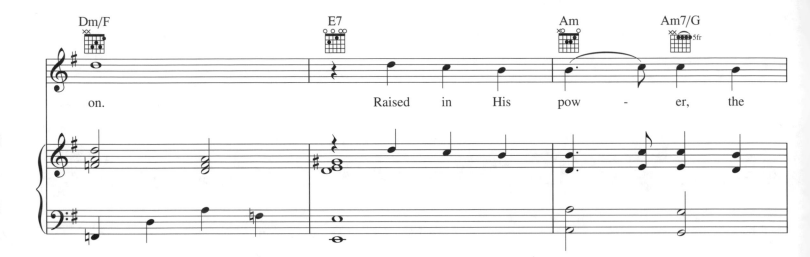

on. Raised in His pow - er, the

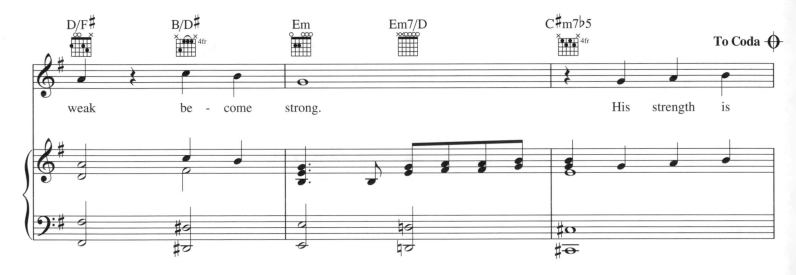

weak be - come strong. His strength is

To Coda ⊕

per - fect, His strength is per - fect. _____

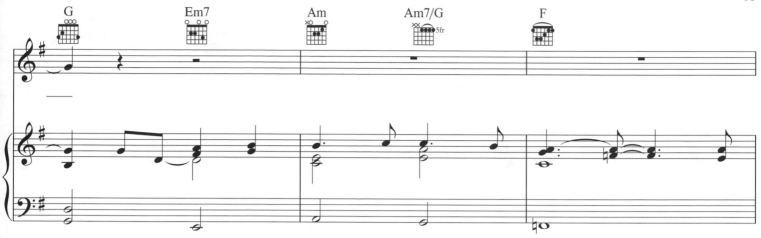

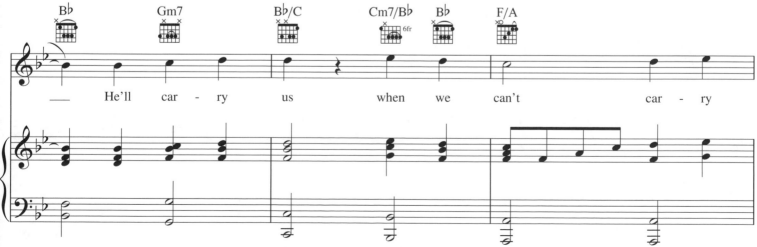

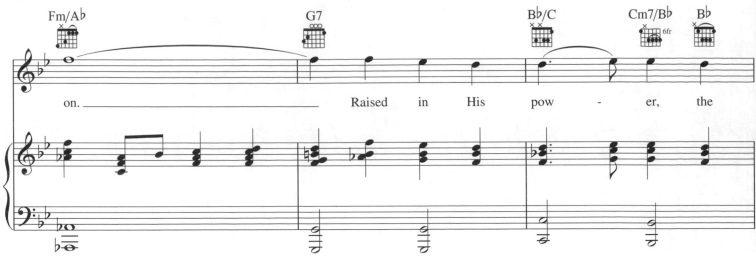

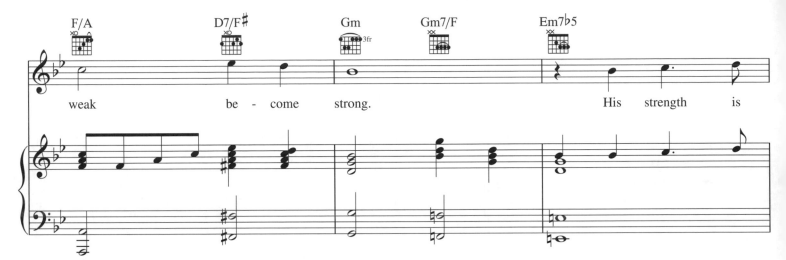

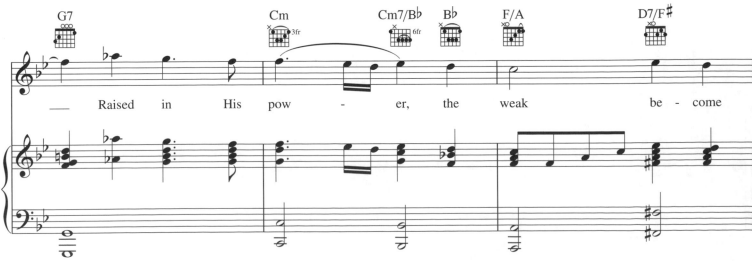

strong, _____ (be - come strong.) _____

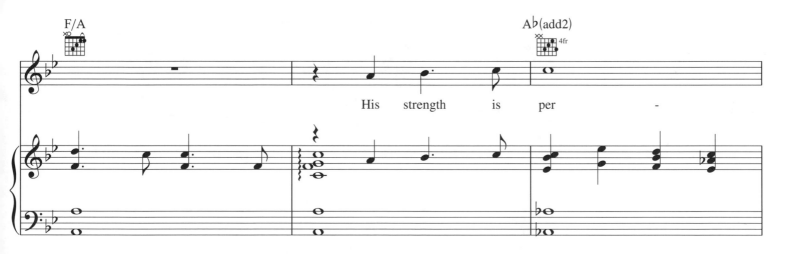

_____ His strength is per - fect, _____

His strength is per -

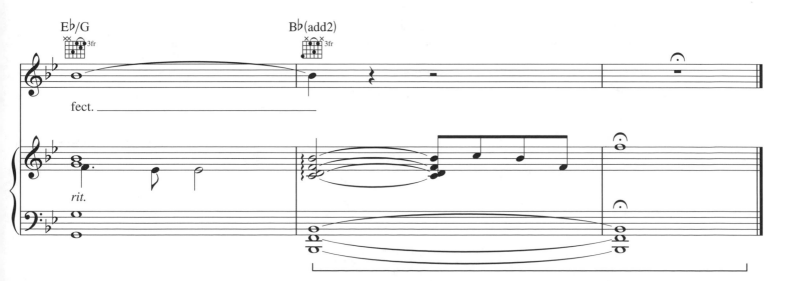

fect. _____

rit.

HOLD ME JESUS

Words and Music by
RICH MULLINS

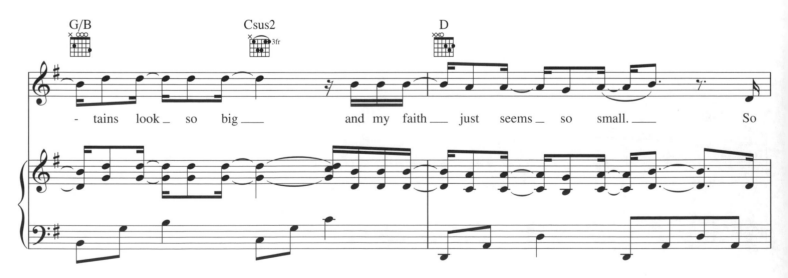

*Recorded a half step lower.

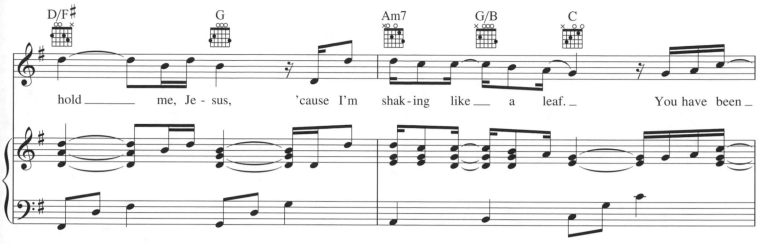

hold _____ me, Je - sus, 'cause I'm shak-ing like _ a leaf. _ You have been _

_ King of _ my _ glo - ry, won't You be _____ my Prince _ of peace? _

_ And I wake _

_ up in _ the night _ and feel _ the dark. _ It's so hot _

_____ in - side _____ my soul, _____ I swear there must be _____ blis - ters on _____ my heart. _____ So

hold _____ me, Je - sus, 'cause I'm shak - ing like _____ a leaf. _____ You have been _____

_____ King of _____ my _____ glo - ry, won't You be _____ my Prince _____ of peace? _____

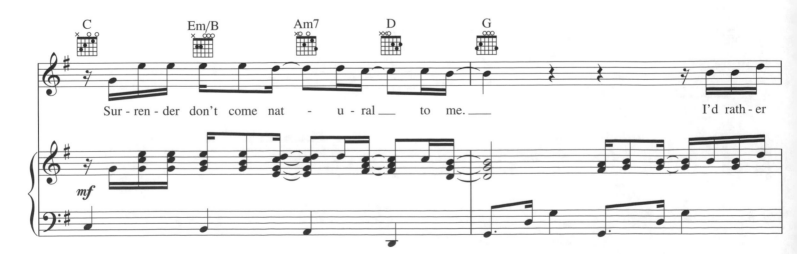

Sur - ren - der don't come nat - u - ral _____ to me. _____ I'd rath - er

fight You for some-thing I don't __ real - ly want __ than to take __ what You give __ that I need. And I've beat __

__ my head __ a - gainst so man - y walls, now I'm fall - ing down, I'm fall - ing __ on __ my __

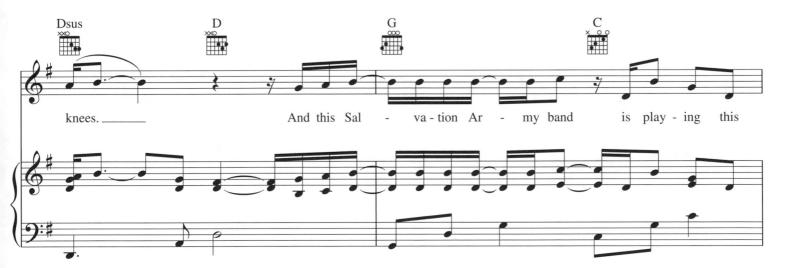

knees. _____ And this Sal - va - tion Ar - my band is play - ing this

hymn. And Your grace __ rings out __ so deep __ it makes my re -

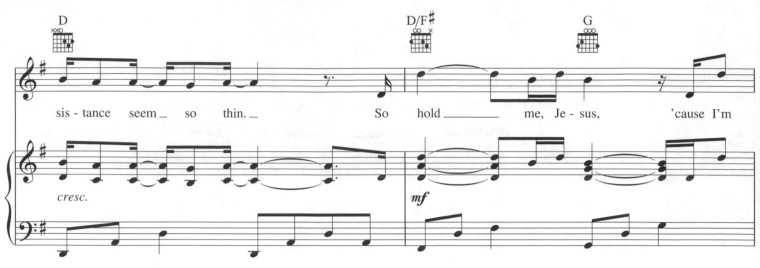

sis - tance seem _ so thin. _ So hold _____ me, Je - sus, 'cause I'm

cresc.

mf

shak - ing like _ a leaf. _ You have been _ King of _ my _ glo - ry, won't You be _

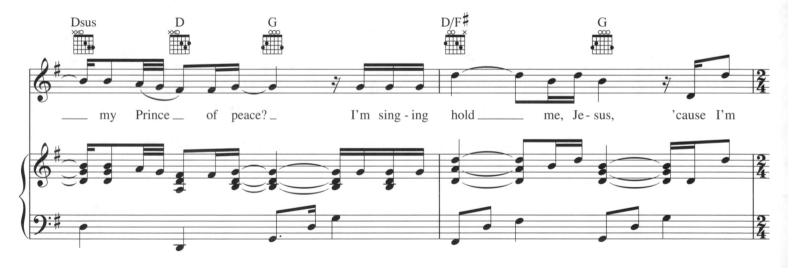

_ my Prince _ of peace? _ I'm sing - ing hold _____ me, Je - sus, 'cause I'm

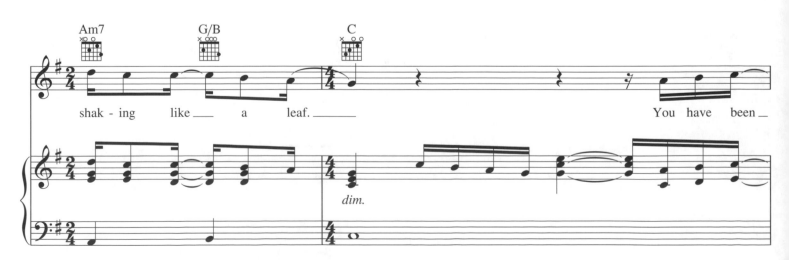

shak - ing like _ a leaf. _____ You have been _

dim.

King of __ my __ glo - ry, won't You be ____ my Prince __ of peace? __ You have been __

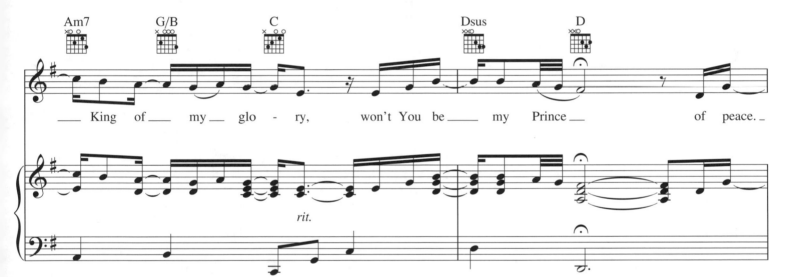

King of __ my __ glo - ry, won't You be ____ my Prince __ of peace. __

HOW BEAUTIFUL

Words and Music by
TWILA PARIS

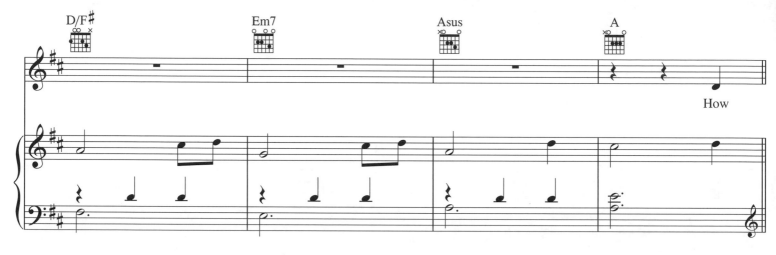

beau - ti - ful _____ the hands _____ that _ served _____ the
beau - ti - ful _____ the heart _____ that _ bled, _____ that
beau - ti - ful _____ the ra - diant _ Bride _____ who

wine and the bread _____ and the sons _ of the earth. How _
took all my _ sin and _ bore _ it in - stead. How _
waits for her _ Groom with His light _ in her eyes. How _

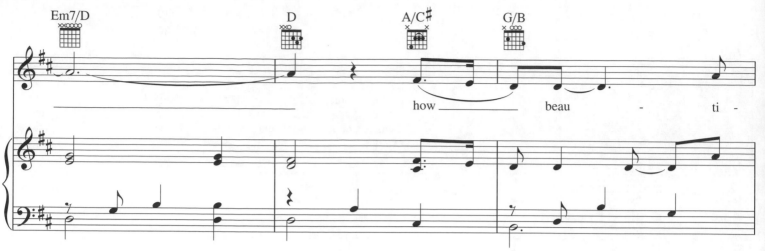

how _____ beau - ti -

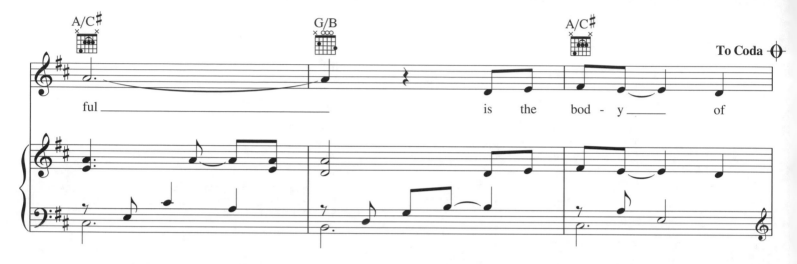

ful _____ is the bod - y _____ of

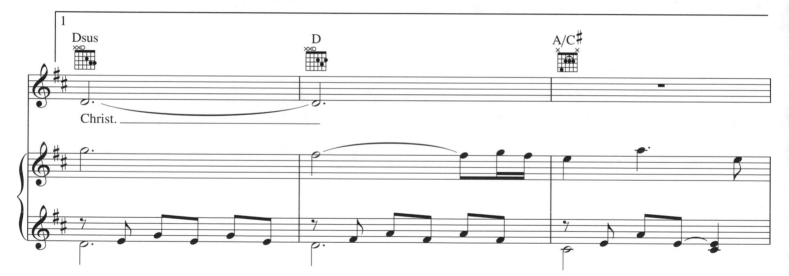

Christ. _____

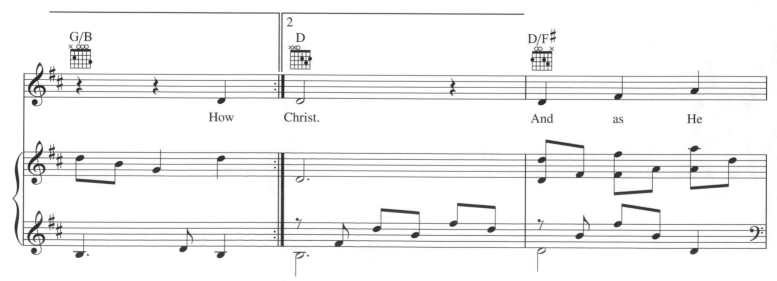

How Christ. And as He

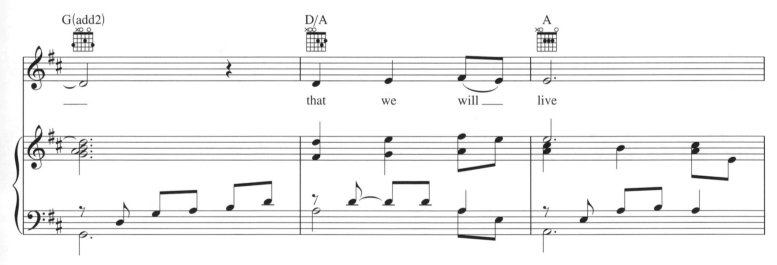

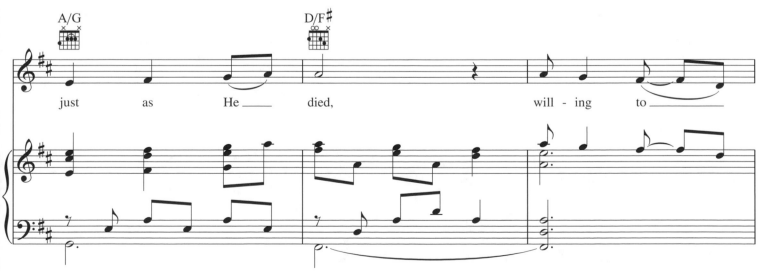

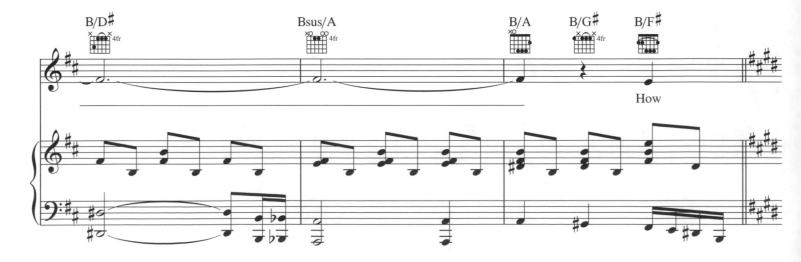

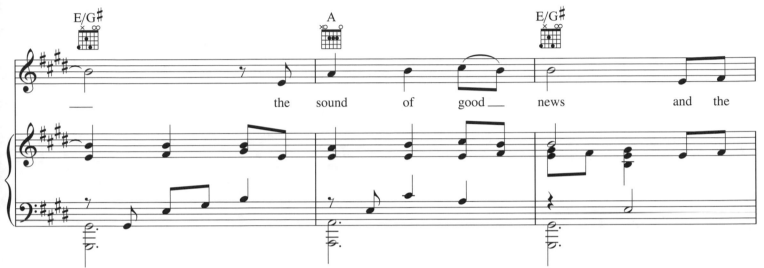

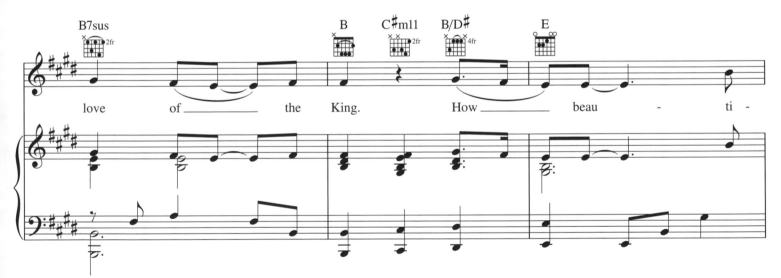

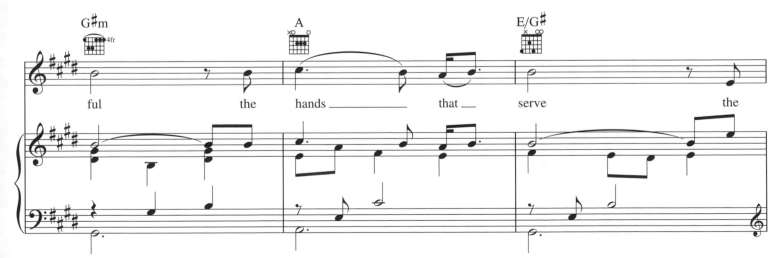

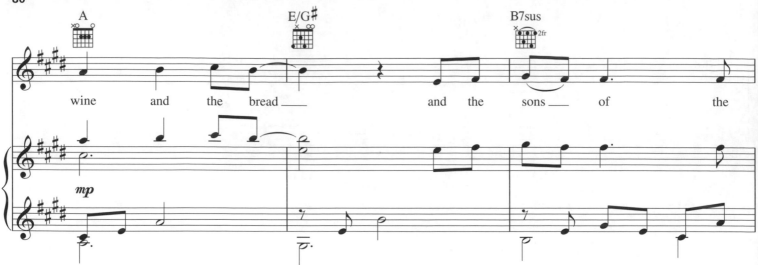

wine and the bread _____ and the sons _____ of the

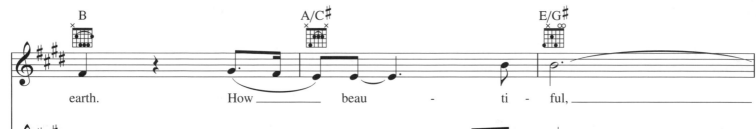

earth. How _____ beau - ti - ful, _____

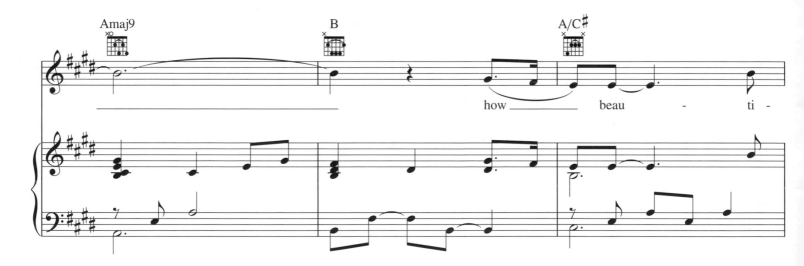

_____ how _____ beau - ti -

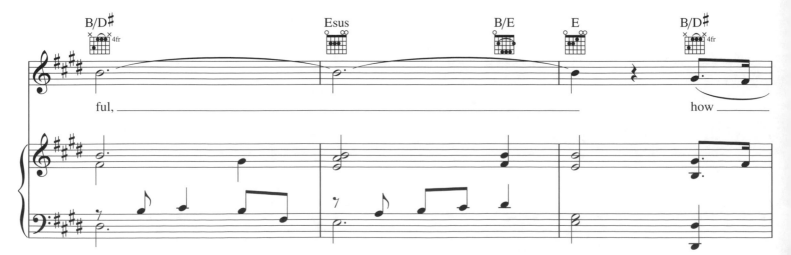

ful, _____ how _____

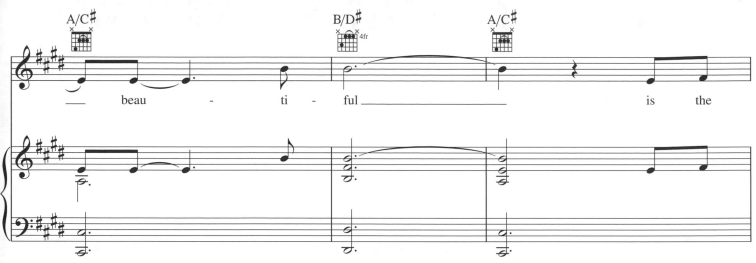

beau - ti - ful _____ is the

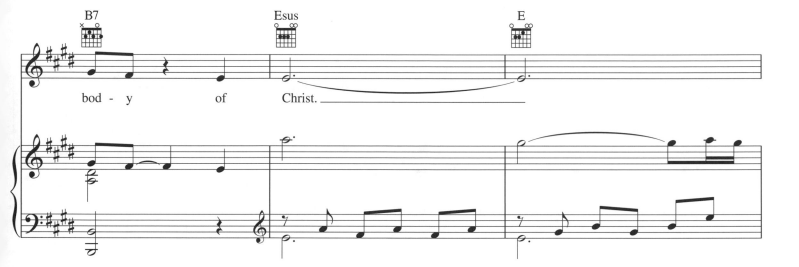

bod - y of Christ. _____

rit.

HOW EXCELLENT IS THY NAME

Words and Music by DICK TUNNEY,
MELODIE TUNNEY and PAUL SMITH

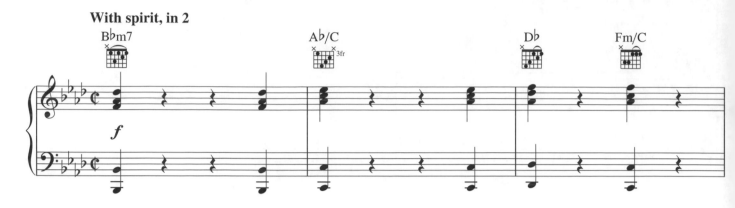

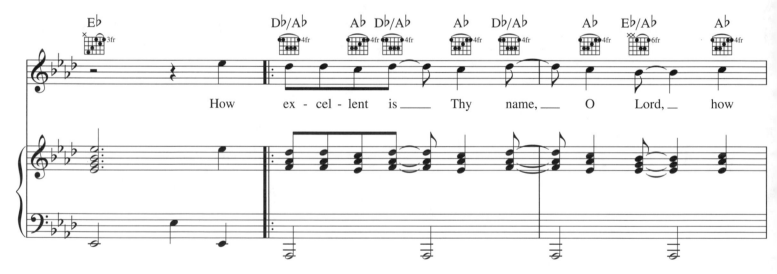

How ex-cel-lent is___ Thy name,___ O Lord,___ how

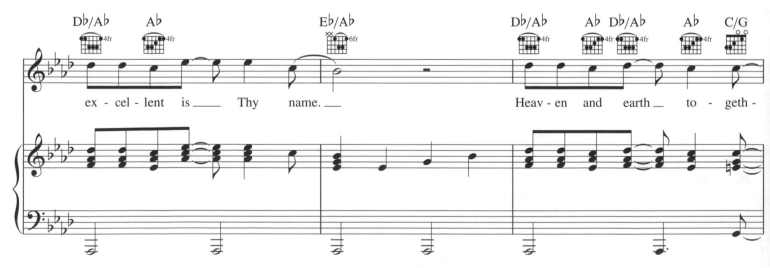

ex-cel-lent is___ Thy name.___ Heav-en and earth___ to-geth-

Cre - a - tion shows __ Your splen - dor, Your

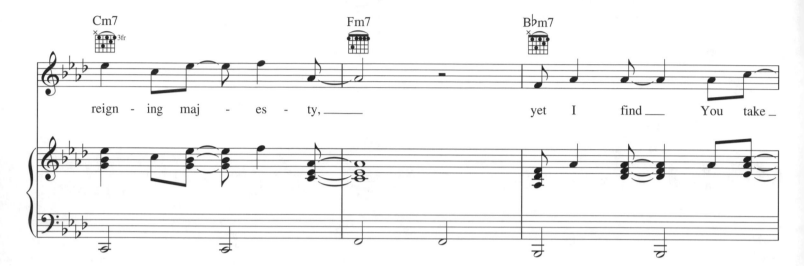

reign - ing maj - es - ty, _____ yet I find __ You take __

__ the time __ to care for one __ like me. _____ How

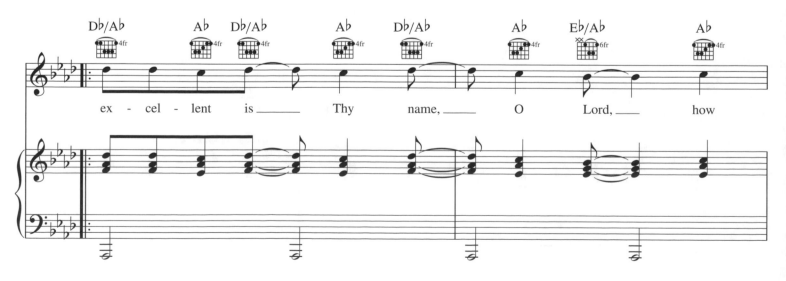

ex - cel - lent is _____ Thy name, _____ O Lord, ____ how

cho-sen few ___ will gath - er to pro-claim You Lord ___ Most High. ___

___ With joy - ful hal - le - lu - jahs the

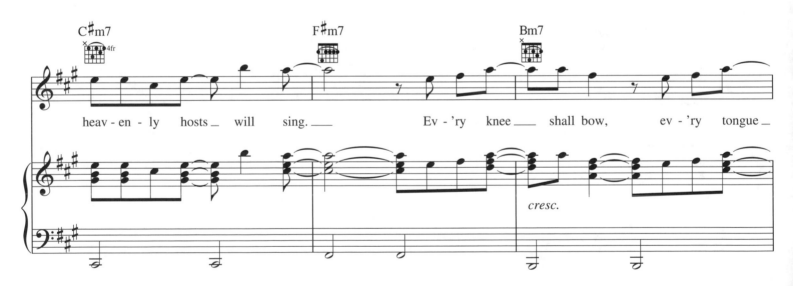

heav - en - ly hosts ___ will sing. ___ Ev - 'ry knee ___ shall bow, ev - 'ry tongue ___

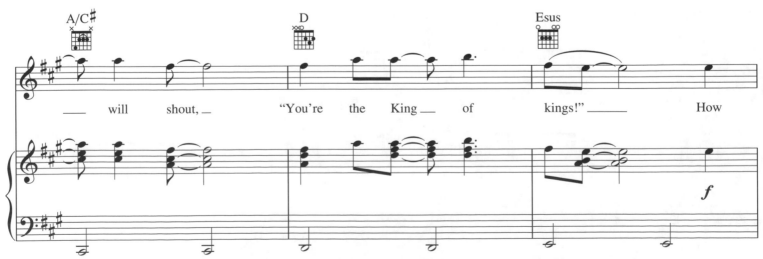

___ will shout, ___ "You're the King ___ of kings!" _____ How

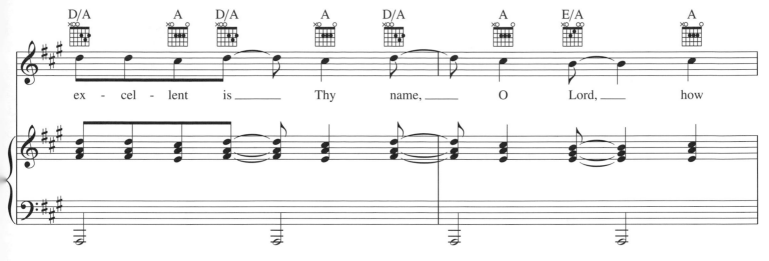

ex - cel - lent is ___ Thy name, ___ O Lord, ___ how

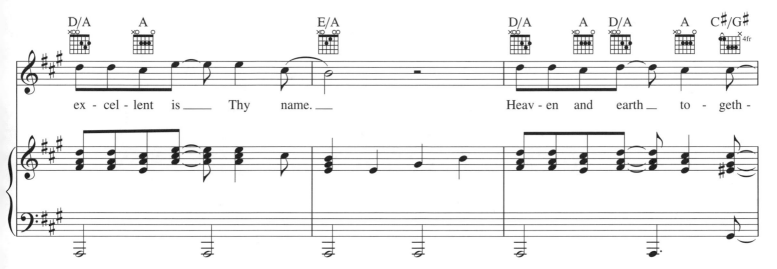

ex - cel - lent is ___ Thy name. ___ Heav - en and earth ___ to - geth -

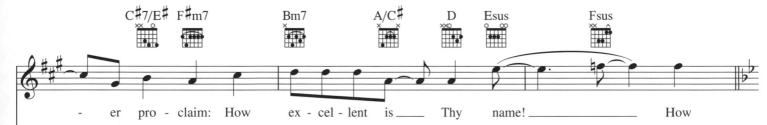

- er pro - claim: How ex - cel - lent is ___ Thy name! _____ How

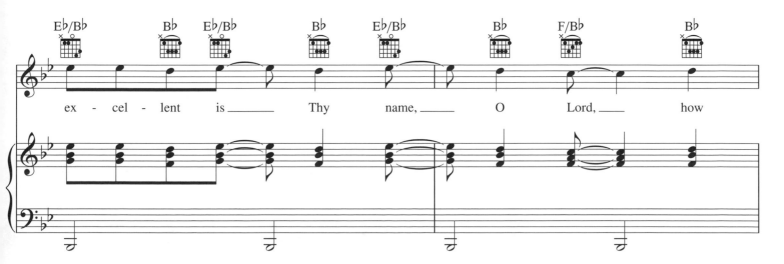

ex - cel - lent is _____ Thy name, ___ O Lord, ___ how

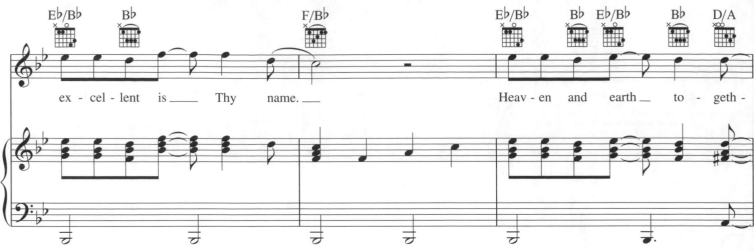

ex - cel - lent is ___ Thy name. ___ Heav - en and earth ___ to - geth -

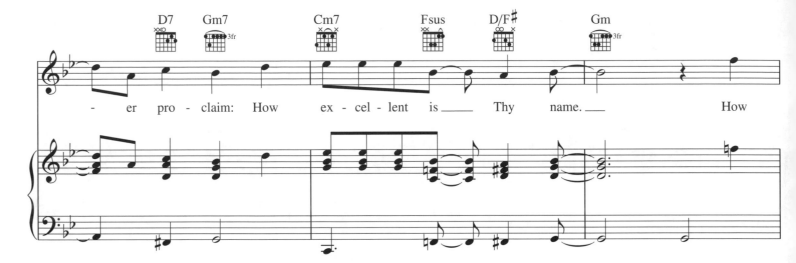

- er pro - claim: How ex - cel - lent is ___ Thy name. ___ How

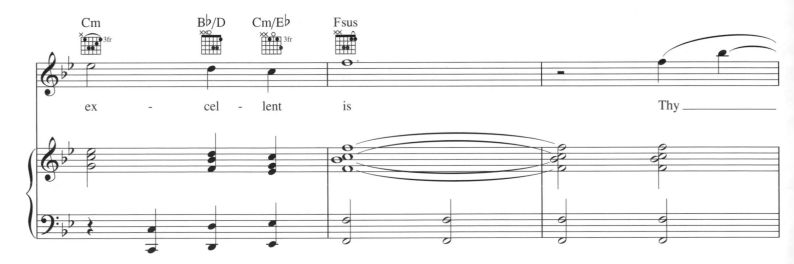

ex - cel - lent is Thy _____

___ name! _____

I AM NOT ASHAMED

Words and Music by
CONSTANT CHANGE

Moderately slow

We're an an - chor for those __ who are hurt - ing. We're a
mo - ment His hand __ has held mer - cy, for all the love __

har - bor for those ___ who are lost.
___ that He's shown ___ all my life, a sim - ple thanks __

Some - times it's not _____ al - ways eas - y _____ bear - ing
_____ does - n't say _____ how I'm feel - ing; I get

Melody is written one octave higher than sung.

I CAN ONLY IMAGINE

Words and Music by
BART MILLARD

mag - ine. ___

Sur - round - ed by ___ Your glo - ry, what

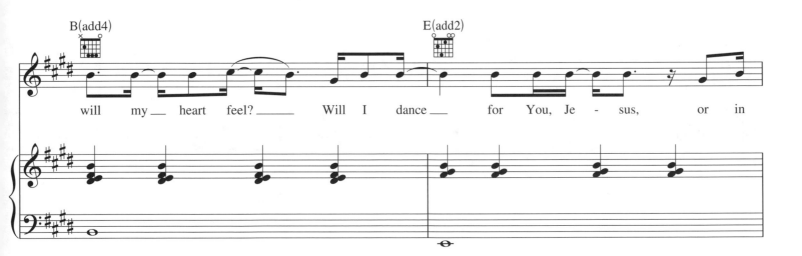

will my ___ heart feel? ___ Will I dance ___ for You, Je - sus, or in

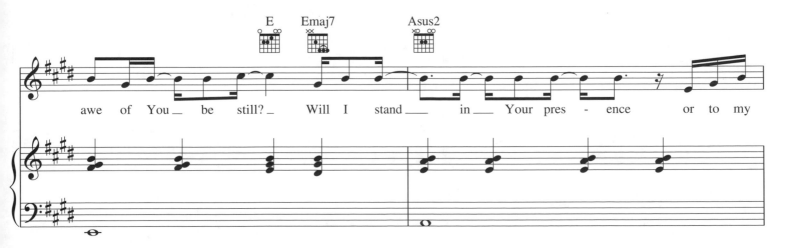

awe of You __ be still? _ Will I stand ___ in ___ Your pres - ence or to my

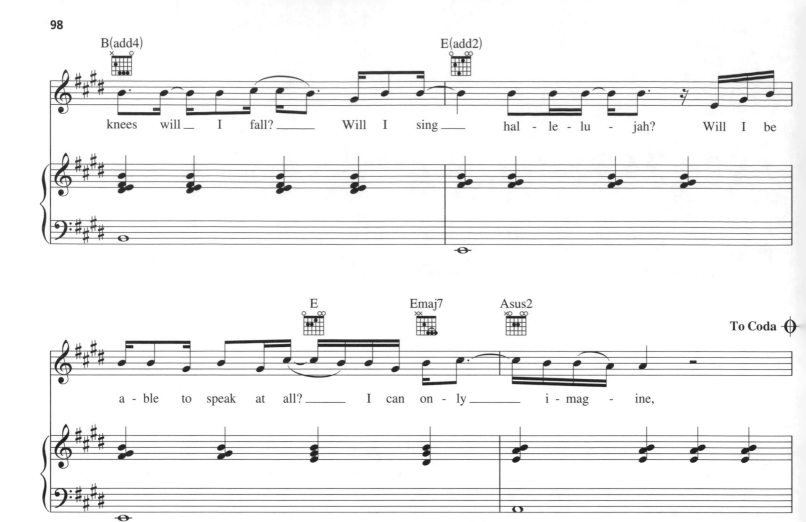

knees will __ I fall? _____ Will I sing ___ hal - le - lu - jah? Will I be

a - ble to speak at all? _____ I can on - ly _____ i - mag ___ - ine,

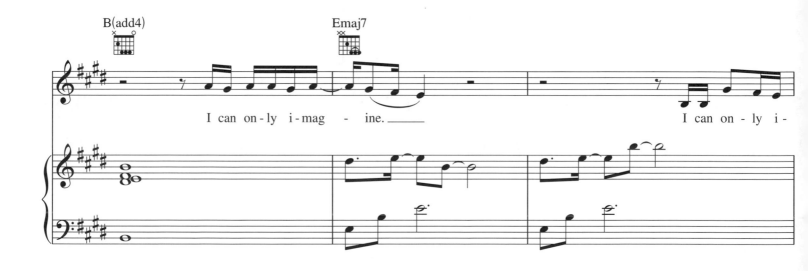

I can on - ly i - mag ___ - ine. _____ I can on - ly i -

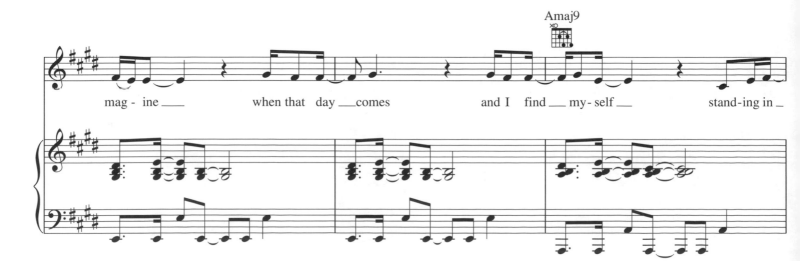

mag - ine ____ when that day ___ comes and I find ___ my - self ___ stand-ing in __

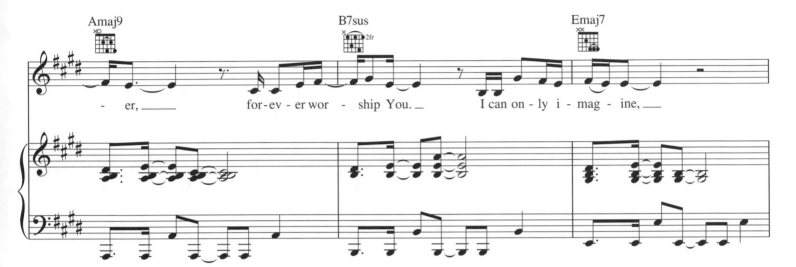

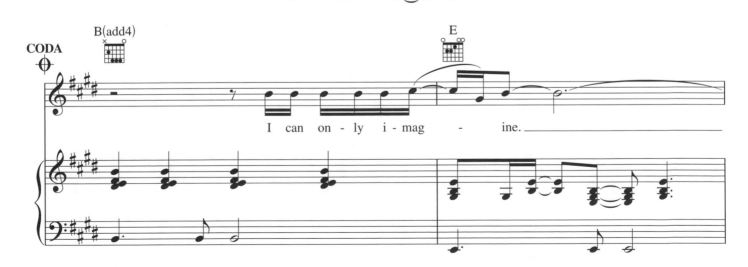

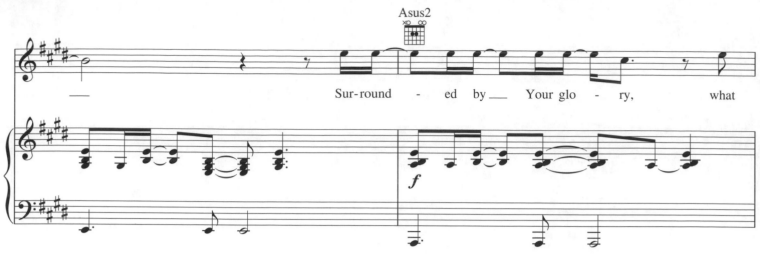

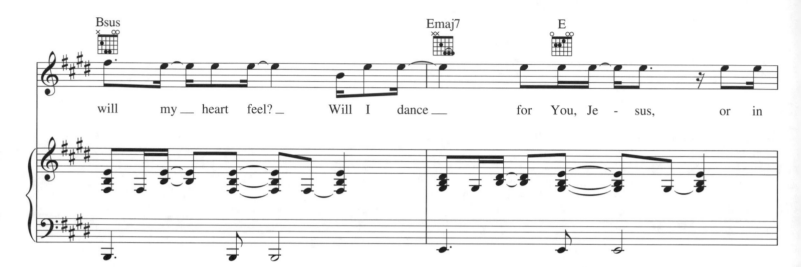

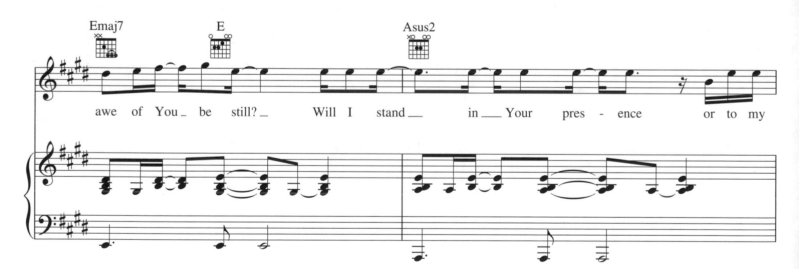

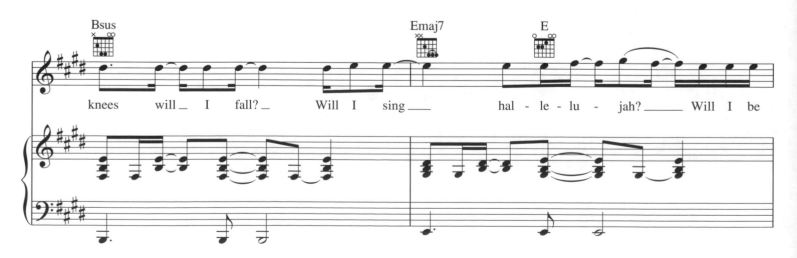

I SURRENDER ALL

Words and Music by DAVID MOFFITT
and REGIE HAMM

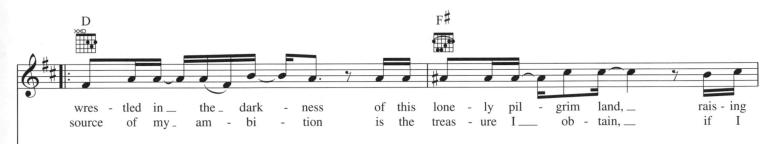

I have

wres - tled in __ the __ dark - ness of this lone - ly pil - grim land, __ rais - ing
source of my __ am - bi - tion is the treas - ure I __ ob - tain, __ if I

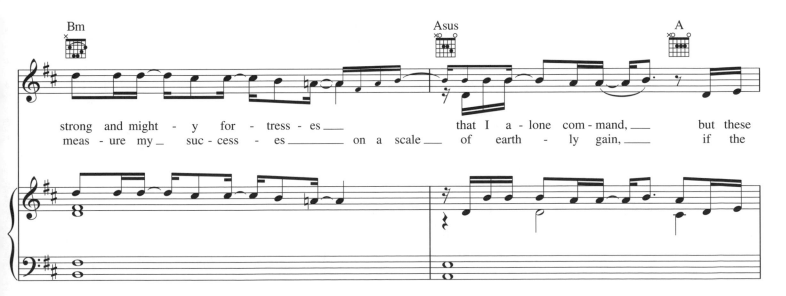

strong and might - y for - tress - es __ that I a - lone com - mand, __ but these
meas - ure my __ suc - cess - es __ on a scale __ of earth - ly gain, __ if the

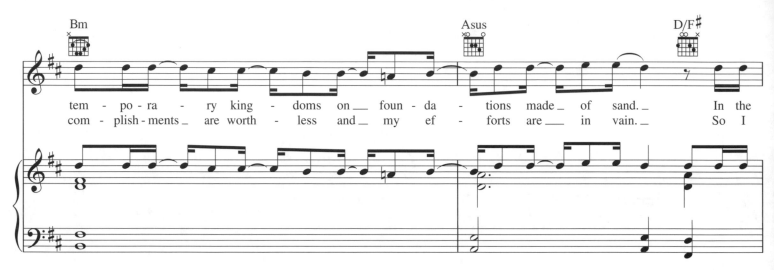

weapons of __ de-fense __ and earth-ly strat-e-gies __ of war, so I'm
ren-der all __ the tri-umph, for it's on-ly by __ Your grace. I re-

lay-ing down __ my arms __ and run-ning help-less-ly __ to Yours. __
lin-quish all __ the glo-ry, I sur-ren-der all __ the praise. __

I sur-ren-der all __ my si-lent hopes __ and dreams, __ though the price __ to

fol-low __ costs me ev-'ry-thing. __ I sur-ren-der

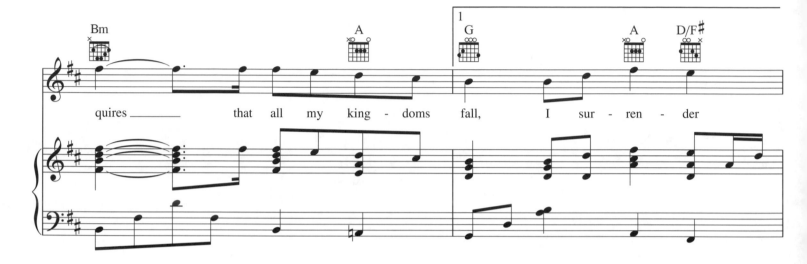

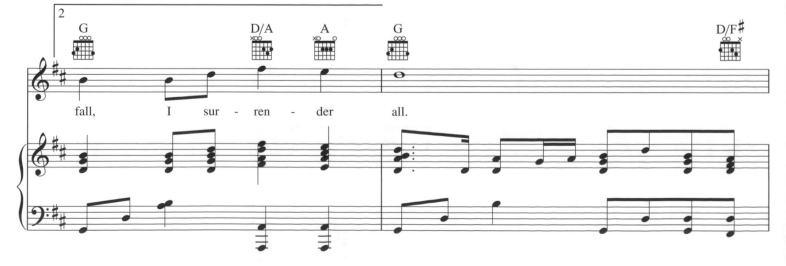

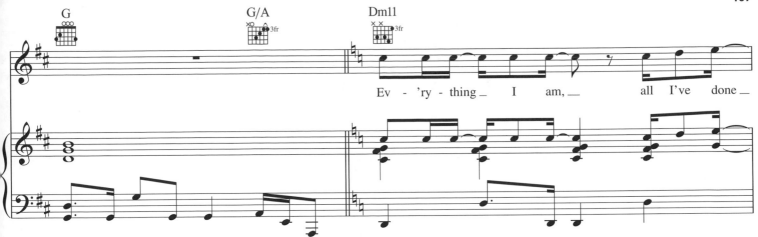

fall, _____ that all my king-doms fall, let all ___ my king-doms ___

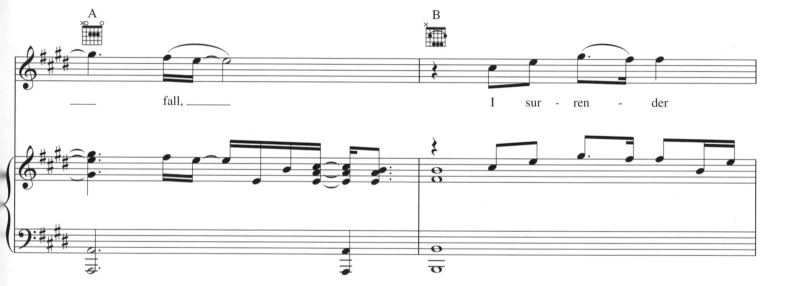

___ fall, _____ I sur-ren-der

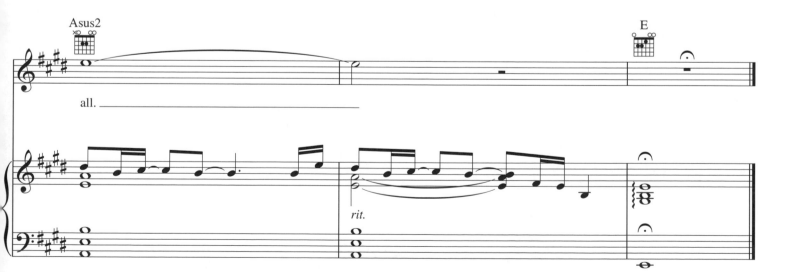

all. _____

IF YOU COULD SEE ME NOW

Words and Music by
KIM NOBLITT

Moderately

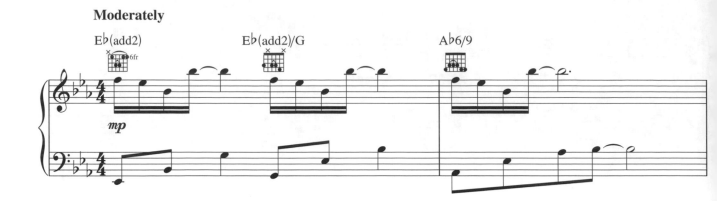

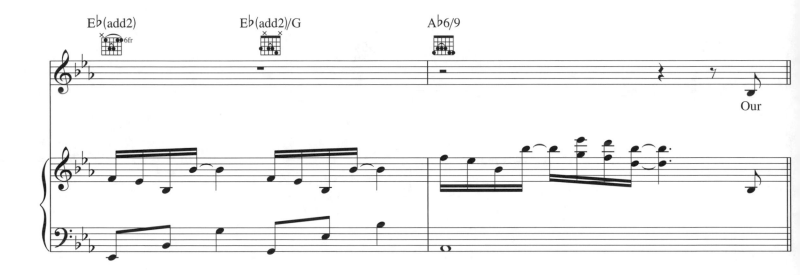

Our

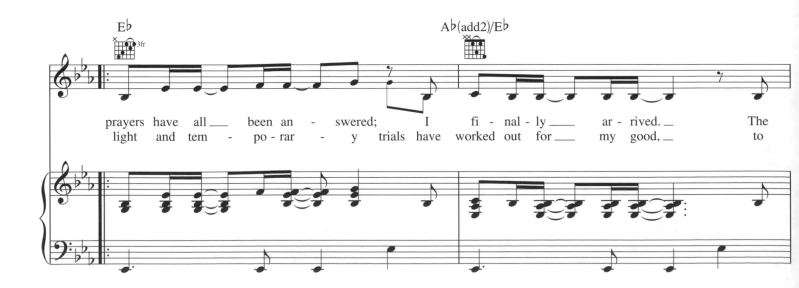

prayers have all ___ been an-swered; I fi-nal-ly ___ ar-rived. ___ The

light and tem - po-rar - - y trials have worked out for ___ my good, ___ to

heal - ing that _____ had been _____ de - layed _____ has now been re - al - ized. _____
know it brought _____ Him glo - ry _____ when I mis - un - der - stood. _____

No one's in _____ a hur - ry, there's no sched - ule _____ to _____ keep. _____ We're
Tho' we've had _____ our sor - rows, they can nev - er _____ com - pare. _____ What

all en - joy - ing Je - sus, just sit - ting at _____ His
Je - sus has _____ in store _____ for us, no lan - guage _____ can

feet. }
share. }   If you could see me now, _____   I'm

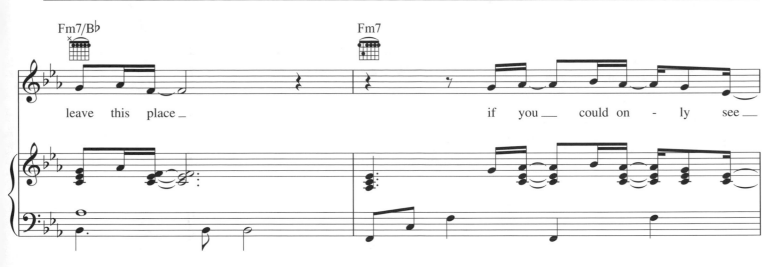

leave this place __ if you __ could on - ly see __

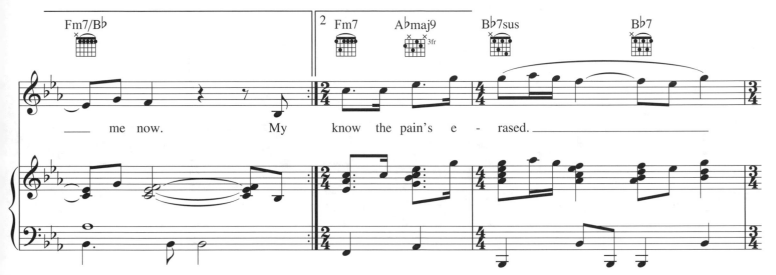

__ me now. My know the pain's e - rased. _____

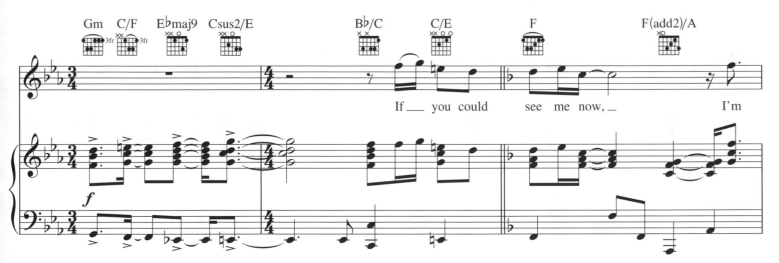

If __ you could see me now, __ I'm

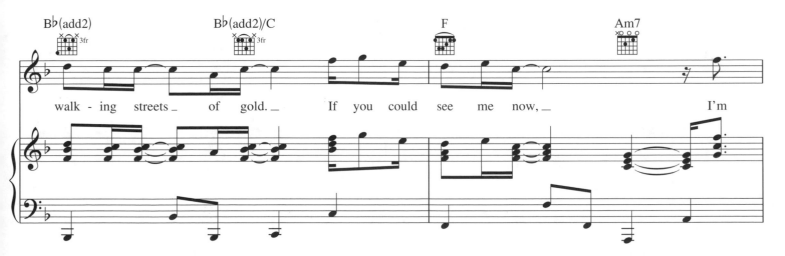

walk - ing streets __ of gold. __ If you could see me now, __ I'm

now,   if you could see ____ me now,

if you could on - ly   see   me ___ now. ___

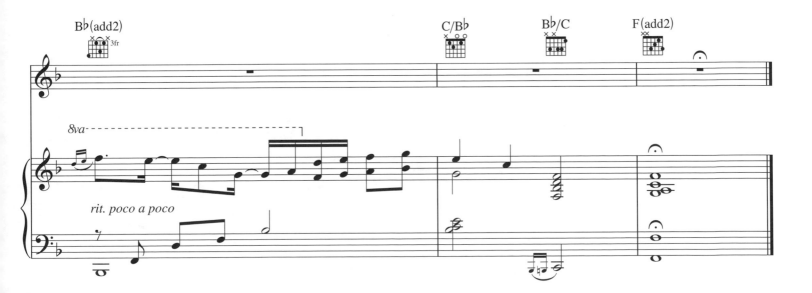

IN HIS PRESENCE

Words and Music by DICK TUNNEY
and MELODIE TUNNEY

With expression

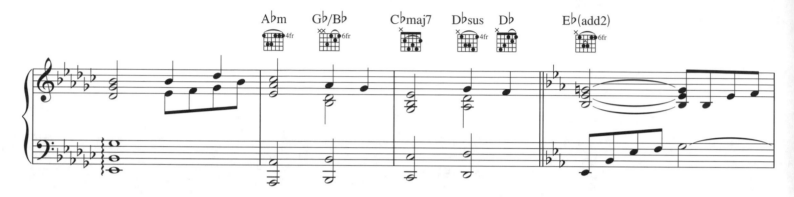

In the qui - et of this hour, as I
be such sweet re - ward when we

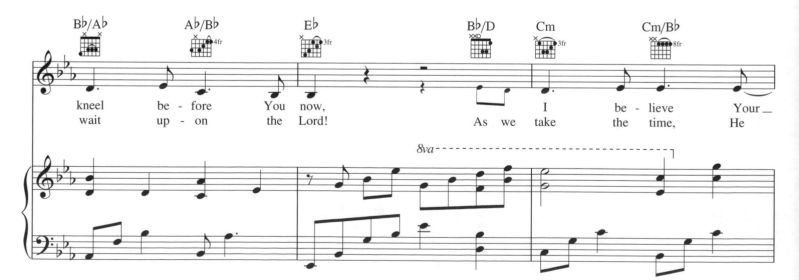

kneel be - fore You now, I be - lieve Your
wait up - on the Lord! As we take the time, He

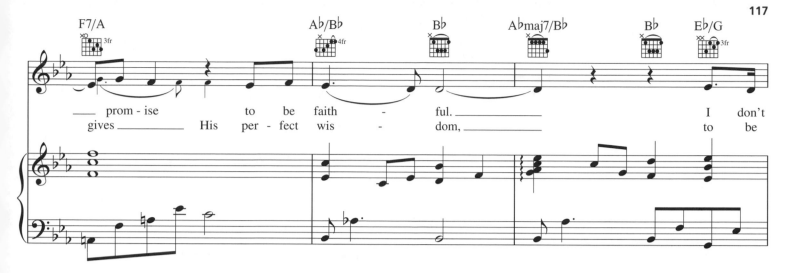

prom - ise to be faith - ful. _____ I don't
gives _____ His per - fect wis - dom, _____ to be

al - ways un - der - stand what Your per - fect will de -
found in Him a - lone. All our deep - est se - crets _____

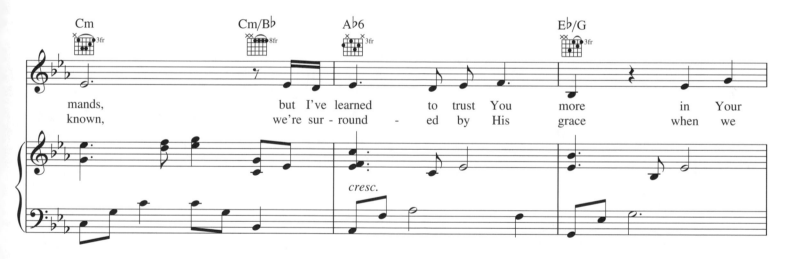

mands, but I've learned to trust You more in Your
known, we're sur - round - ed by His grace when we

cresc.

To Coda ⊕

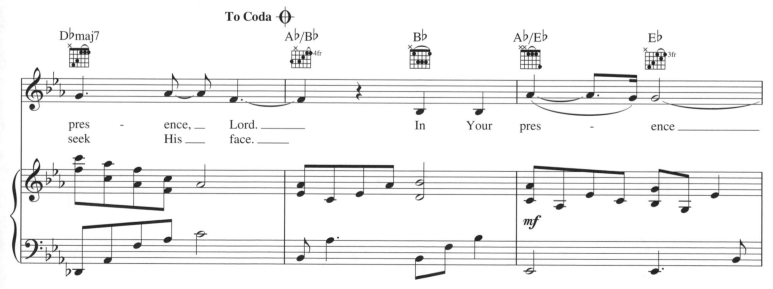

pres - ence, _____ Lord. _____ In Your pres - ence _____
seek His _____ face. _____

mf

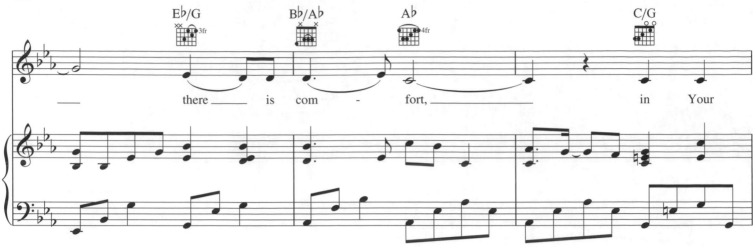

there ___ is com - fort, _____ in Your

pres - ence _____ there is peace. _____

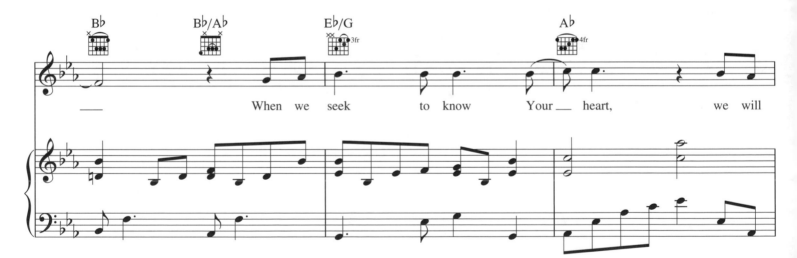

___ When we seek to know Your ___ heart, we will

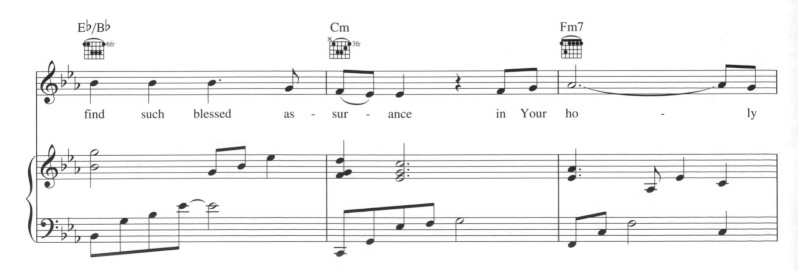

find such blessed as - sur - ance in Your ho - ly

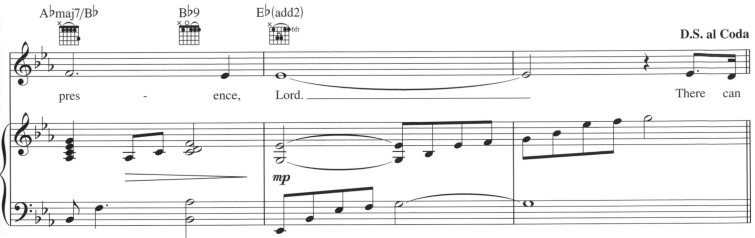

D.S. al Coda

pres - ence, Lord. _____ There can

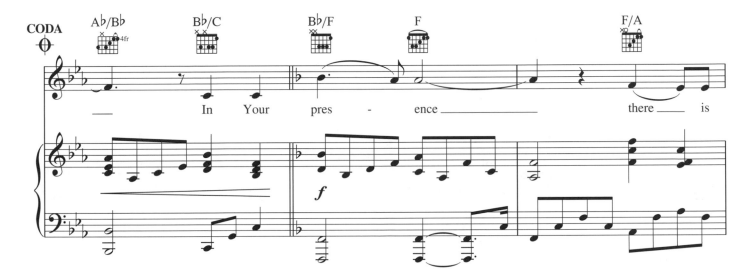

CODA

In Your pres - ence _____ there _____ is

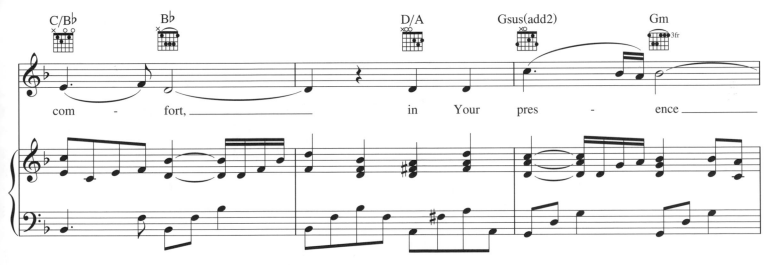

com - fort, _____ in Your pres - ence _____

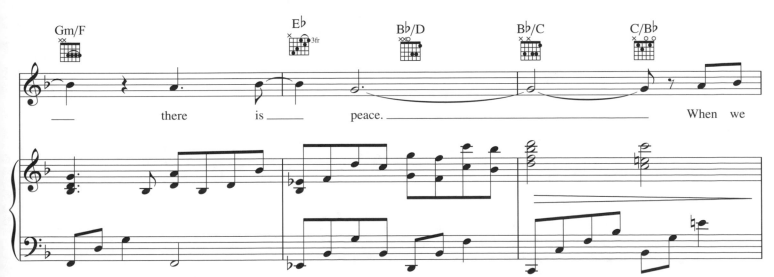

_____ there is _____ peace. _____ When we

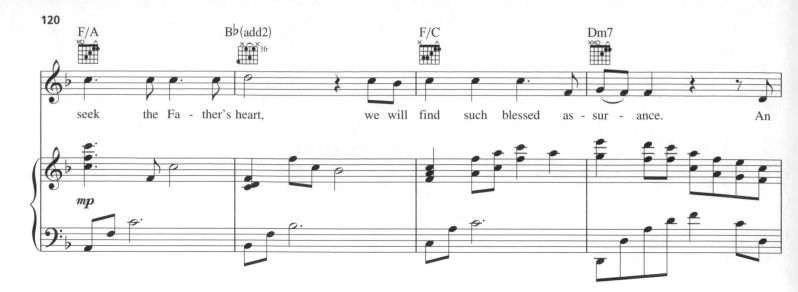

seek the Fa - ther's heart, we will find such blessed as - sur - ance. An

ev - er - o - pen ___ door _____ to know our Sav - ior ___ more, in the

pres - ence of our Lord. _____

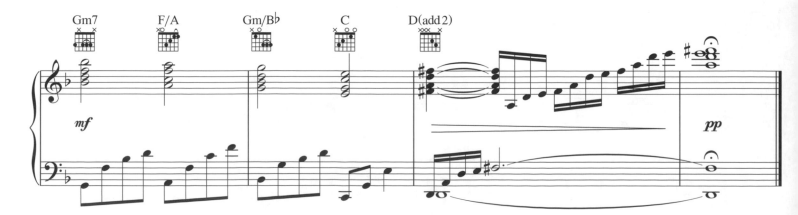

JESUS WILL STILL BE THERE

Words and Music by JOHN MANDEVILLE
and ROBERT STERLING

Slowly

Things change, _ plans fail, _ you look for love _ on a grand-
Time flies, _ hearts turn _ a lit-tle bit wis-er from les-

-er scale. _ Storms rise, _ hopes fade, _ and
-sons learned. _ But some-times _ weak-ness _ wins, _ and

you place your bets _ on _ an-oth-er day.)
you lose your foot-hold _ once _ a-gain.)

When the

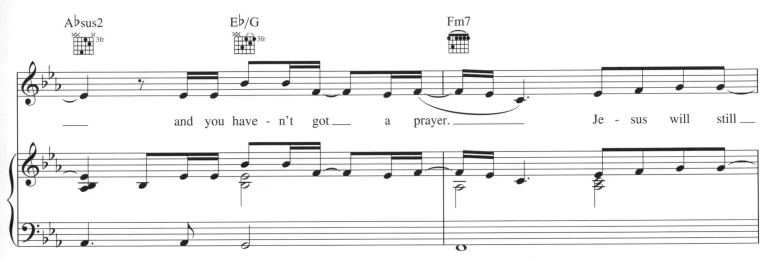

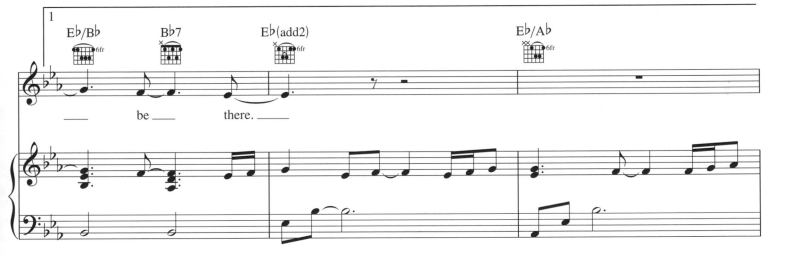

looks like you've lost _____ it all _____ and you have - n't got _____ a prayer, _____

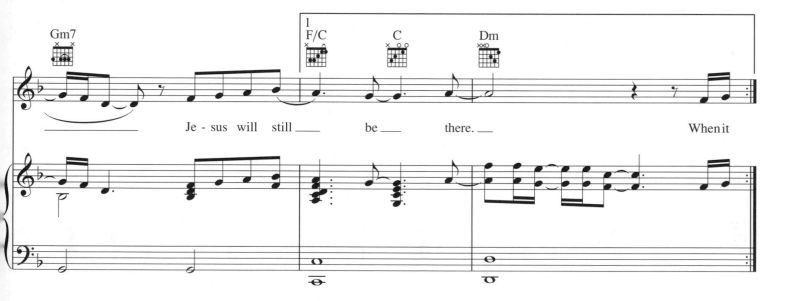

_____ Je - sus will still _____ be _____ there. _____ When it

_____ be _____ there. _____

a tempo

rit.

MORE TO THIS LIFE

Words and Music by STEVEN CURTIS CHAPMAN
and PHIL NAISH

Am7　　　　　　　　　　**Bm7**

hid - den in ____ their eyes. _____ But they all looked back at me ____ as if ____ to say, ____
bet - ter than ____ to - day. _____ But in the morn - ing light ____ it looks ____ the same; ____

C　　　　　　　　　　　　　　**G**

_____ "Life just ____ goes on." ____
_____ life just ____ goes on. ____

C6/9　　　　　　　　　　　　　**G**

The old fa - mil - iar sto - ry, told ____
He takes care of ____ his fam - 'ly, takes ____

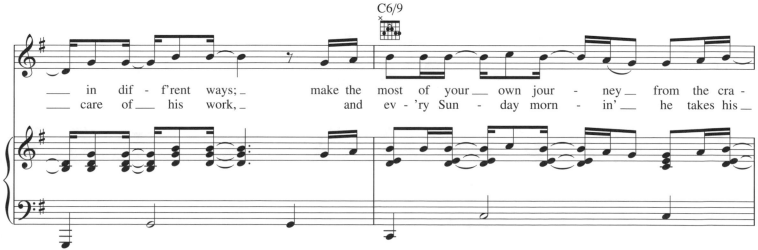

C6/9

____ in dif - f'rent ways; ____ make the most of your ____ own jour - ney ____ from the cra -
____ care of ____ his work, ____ and ev - 'ry Sun - day morn - in' ____ he takes his ____

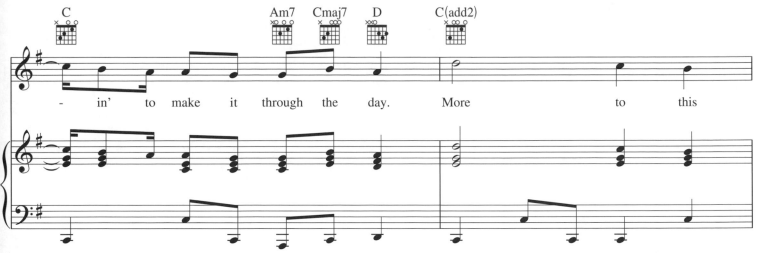

-in' to make it through the day. More to this

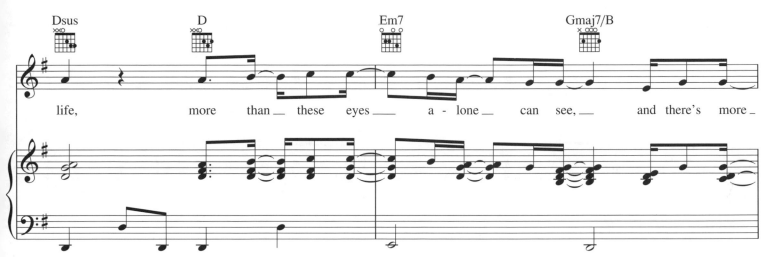

life, more than these eyes a - lone can see, and there's more

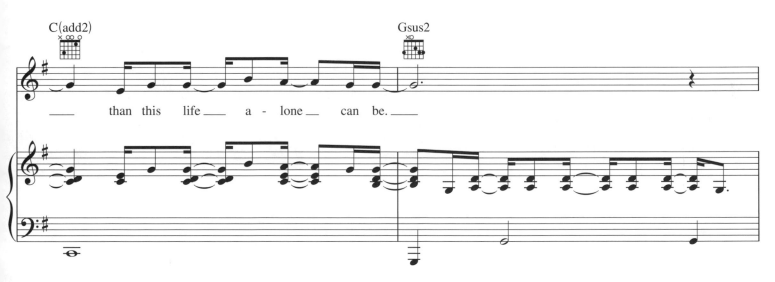

than this life a - lone can be.

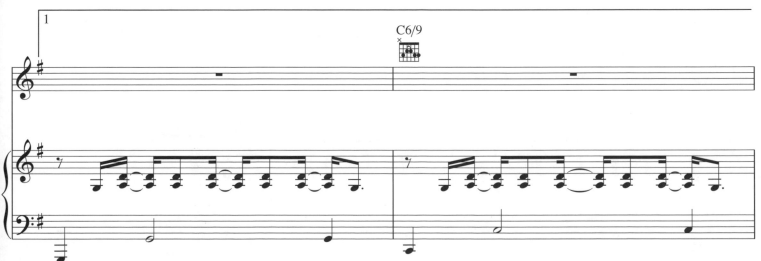

To -   So

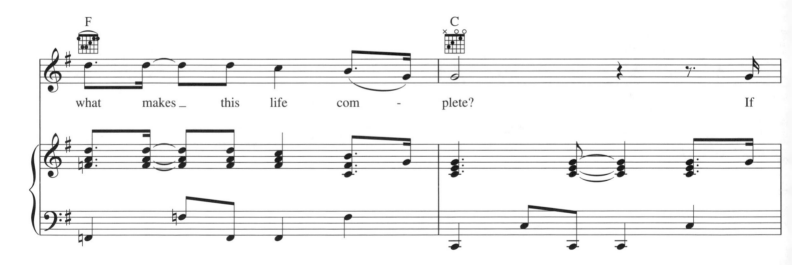

Am7   Bm   G/B

where do ___ we start ___   to find ev - 'ry part ___   of

F   C

what makes ___ this life com - plete?   If

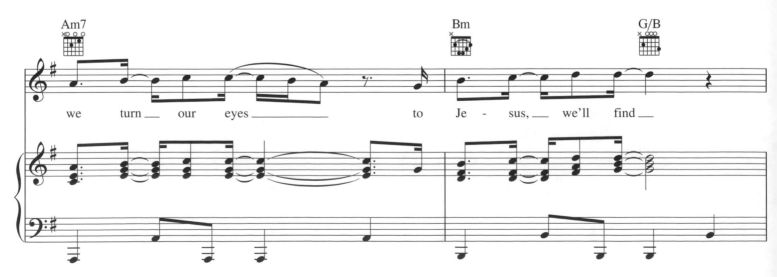

Am7   Bm   G/B

we turn ___ our eyes _____   to Je - sus, ___ we'll find ___

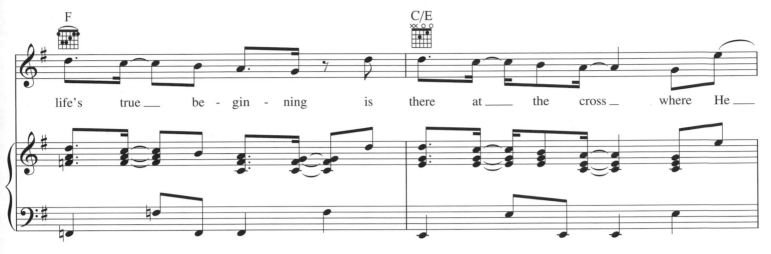

life's true ___ be - gin - ning is there at ___ the cross ___ where He ___

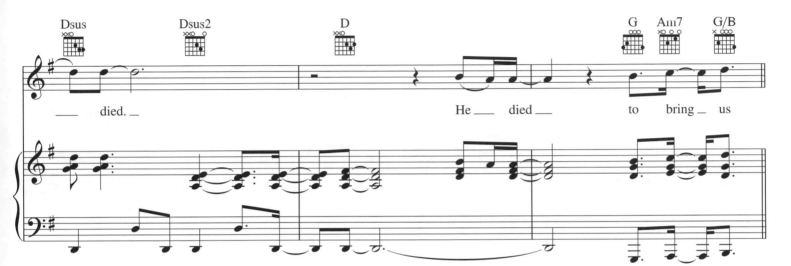

___ died. ___ He ___ died ___ to bring ___ us

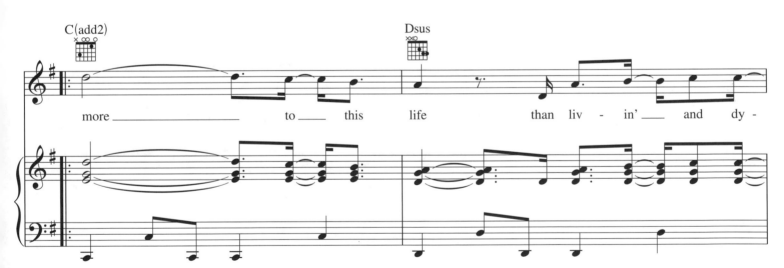

more _____ to ___ this life than liv - in' ___ and dy -

- in', more than ___ just try - in' to make it through the day.

More to this life, more than these eyes

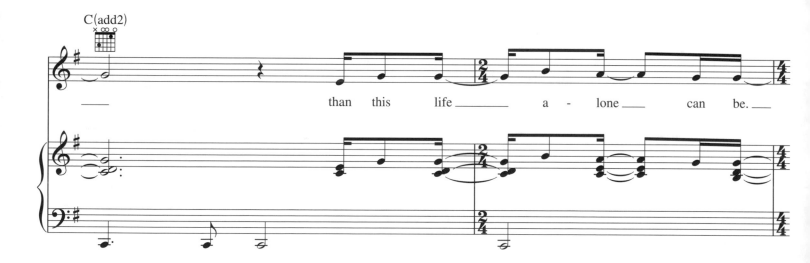

1
a - lone can see. And there's

2
a - lone can see, and there's more

than this life a - lone can be.

More to ___ this

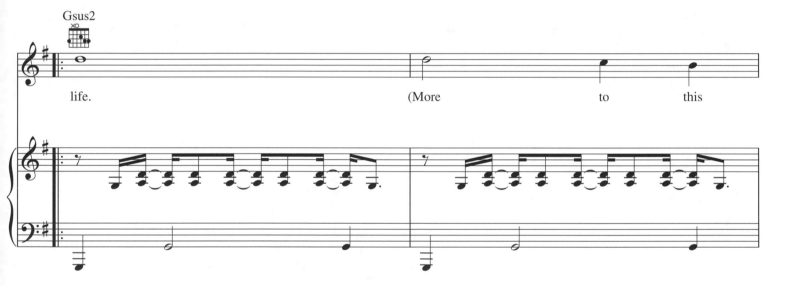

life. (More to this

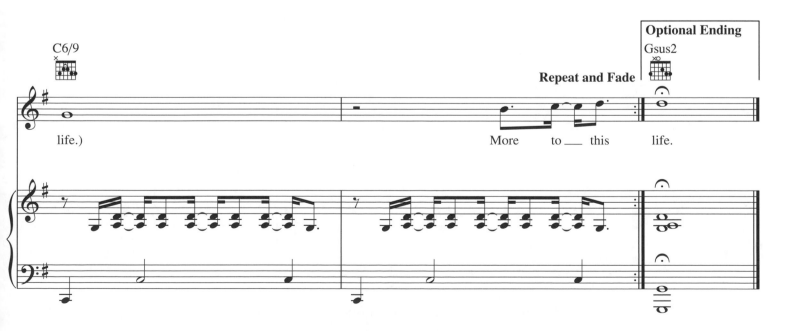

life.) More to ___ this life.

PEOPLE NEED THE LORD

Words and Music by PHILL McHUGH
and GREG NELSON

Tenderly

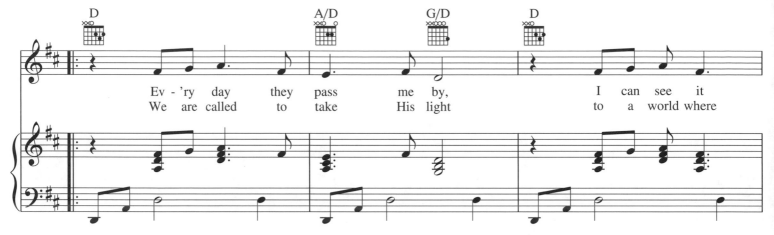

Ev - 'ry day they pass me by, I can see it
We are called to take His light to a world where

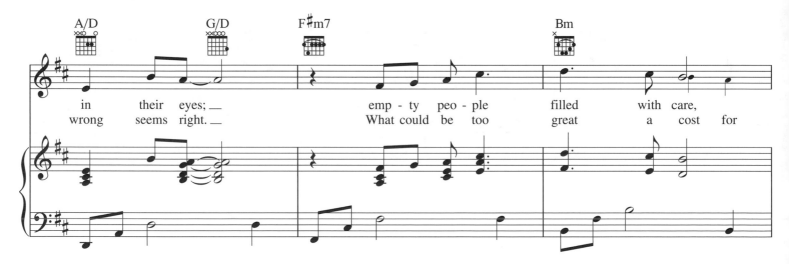

in their eyes; __ emp - ty peo - ple filled with care,
wrong seems right. __ What could be too great a cost for

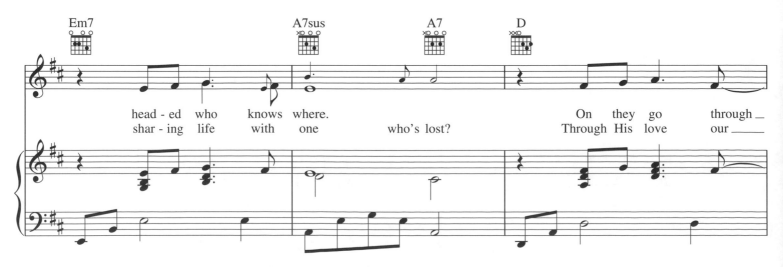

head - ed who knows where. On they go through __
shar - ing life with one who's lost? Through His love our __

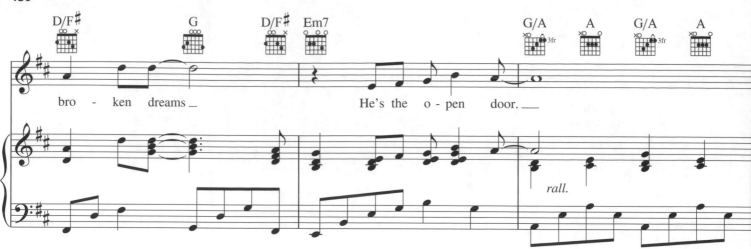

bro - ken dreams ___ He's the o - pen door. ___

Peo - ple need the Lord, ___ peo - ple need the Lord. ___

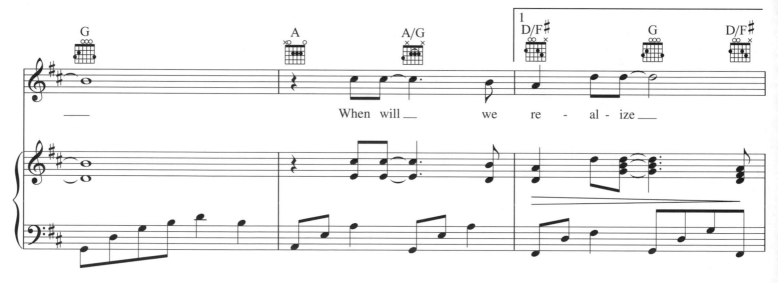

When will ___ we re - al - ize ___

peo - ple need the Lord?

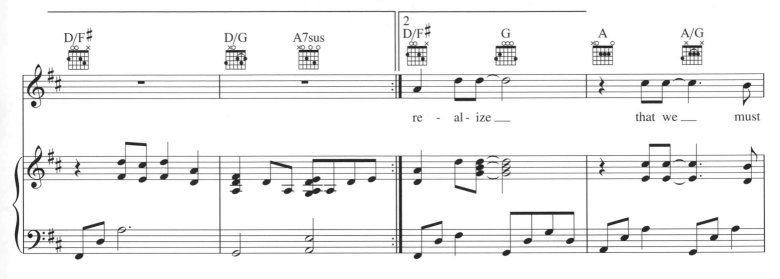

re - al - ize ___ that we ___ must

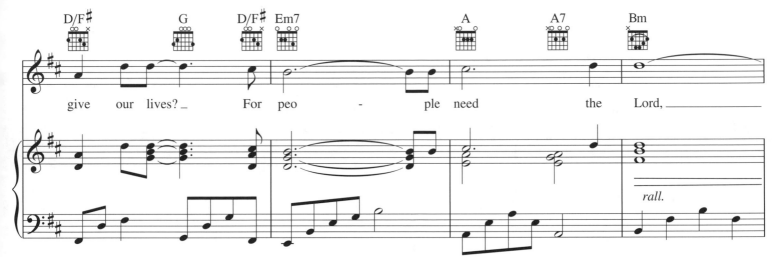

give our lives? ___ For peo - ple need the Lord, ___

rall.

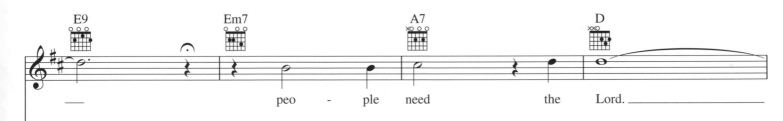

peo - ple need the Lord. ___

slower
mp

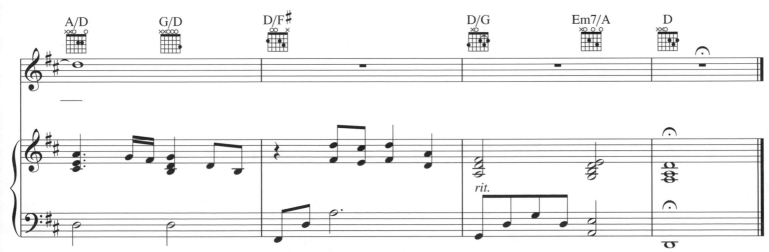

rit.

REDEEMER

Words and Music by
NICOLE C. MULLEN

who _____ showed the moon _____ where to hide _ till eve-
same _____ gen - tle hands _____ that hold me when _ I'm bro-

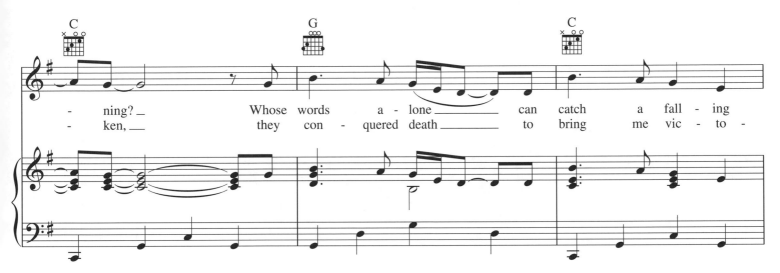

- ning? _ Whose words a - lone _____ can catch a fall - ing
- ken, _ they con - quered death _____ to bring me vic - to -

star? _____ Well, I _____ know } my Re -
ry. _____ Now, I _____ know }

deem - er _____ lives. _____ I _____

know _____ my Re - deem - er lives. _____

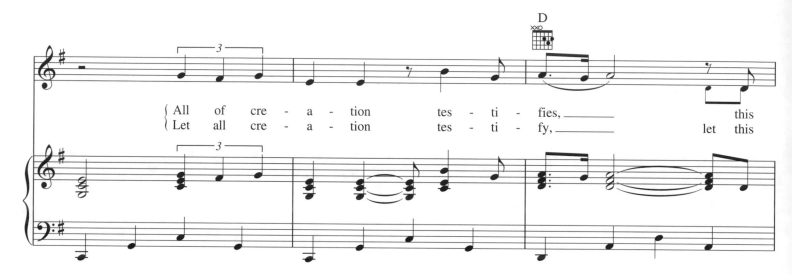

{ All of cre - a - tion tes - ti - fies, _____ this
{ Let all cre - a - tion tes - ti - fy, _____ let this

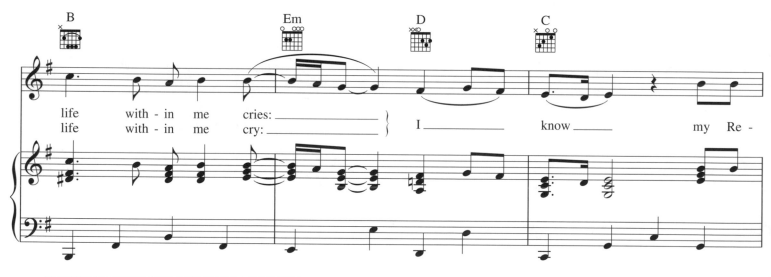

life with - in me cries: _____ } I _____ know _____ my Re -
life with - in me cry: _____

deem - er lives.

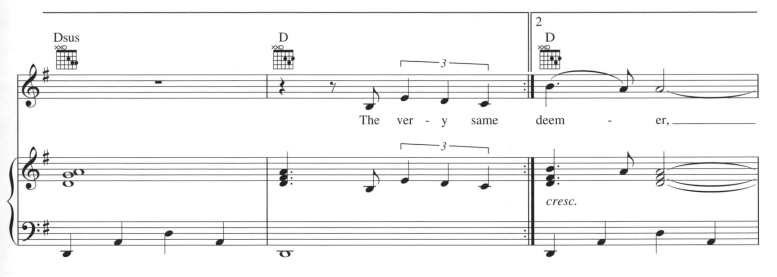

The ver-y same deem-er,___

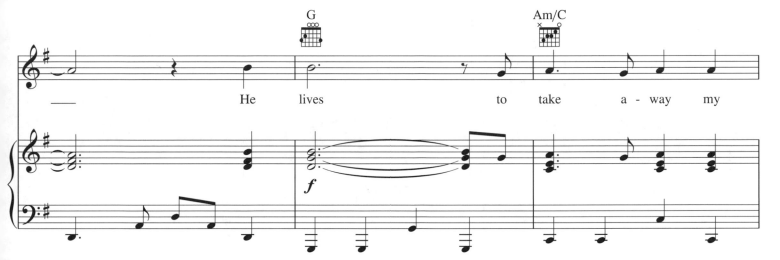

___ He lives to take a-way my

shame.___ And He___ lives; for-

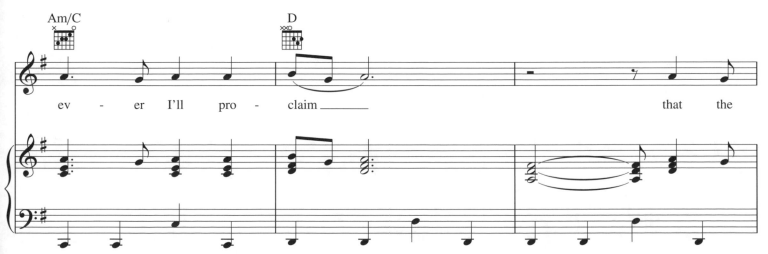

ev-er I'll pro-claim___ that the

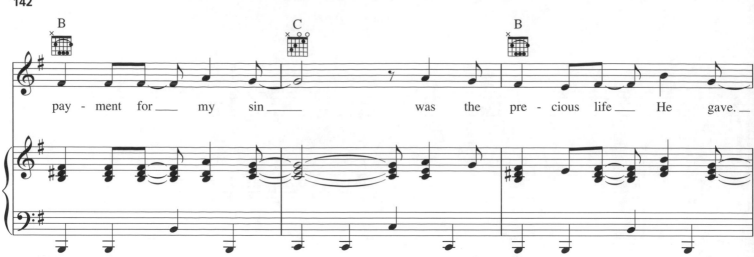

pay - ment for ___ my sin ___ was the pre - cious life ___ He gave. ___

___ But now He's a - live ___ and there's an emp - ty

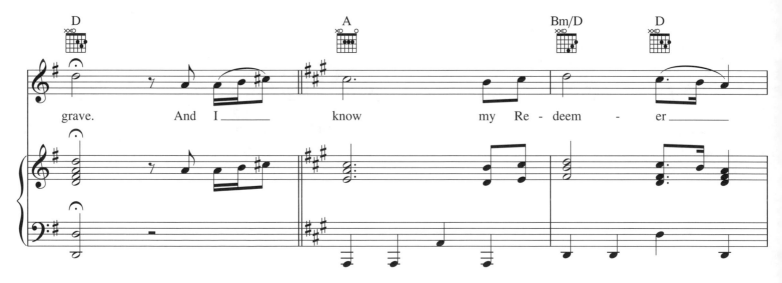

grave. And I ___ know my Re - deem - er ___

lives. ___ I ___ know ___ my Re -

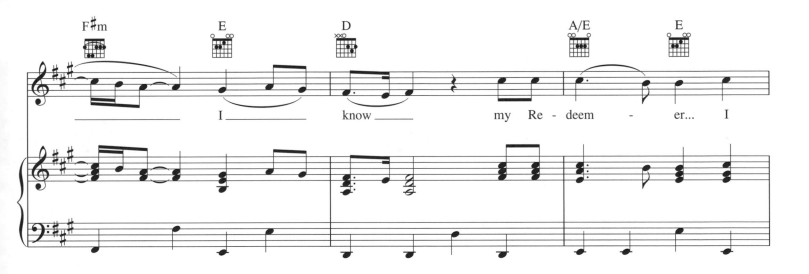

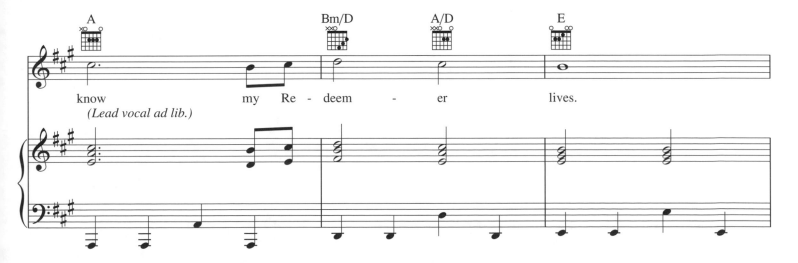

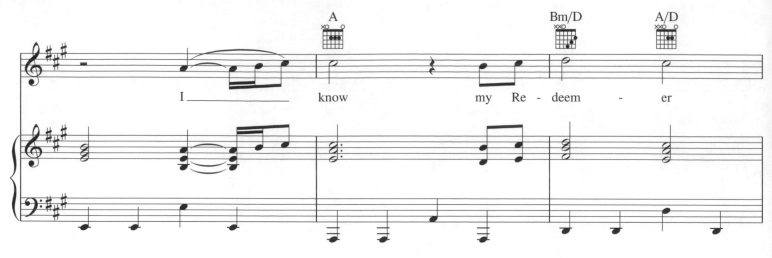

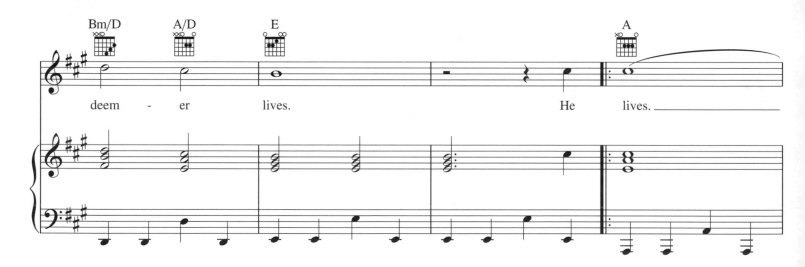

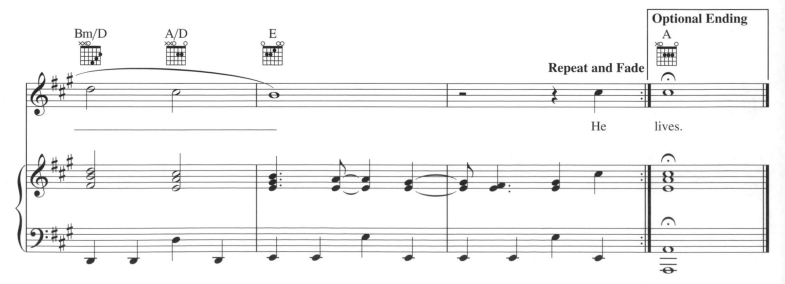

PLACE IN THIS WORLD

Words by WAYNE KIRKPATRICK and AMY GRANT
Music by MICHAEL W. SMITH

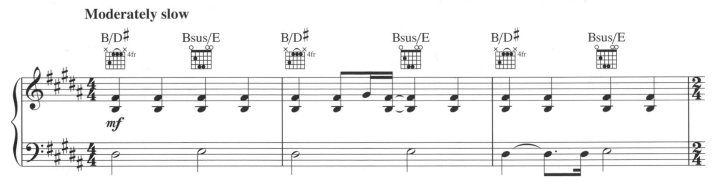

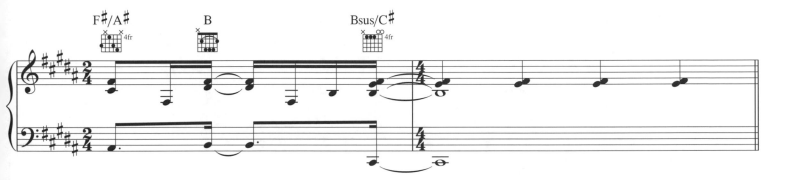

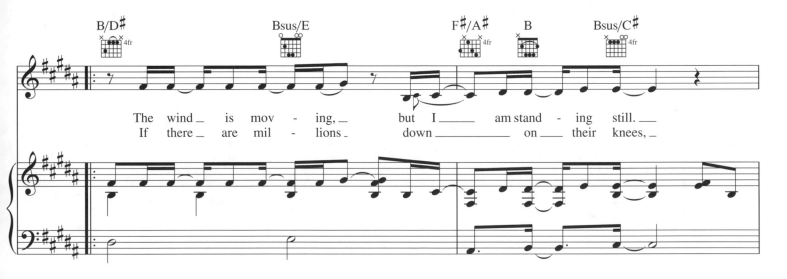

The wind ___ is mov - ing, ___ but I ___ am stand - ing still. ___
If there ___ are mil - lions ___ down _____ on ___ their knees, ___

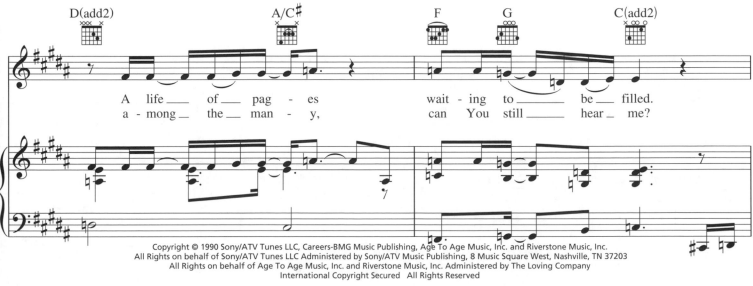

A life ___ of pag - es wait - ing to ___ be ___ filled.
a - mong ___ the ___ man - y, can You still ___ hear ___ me?

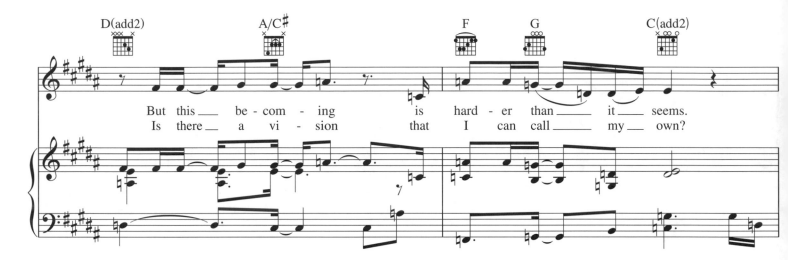

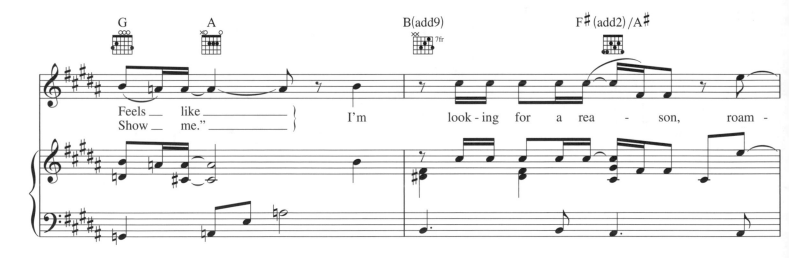

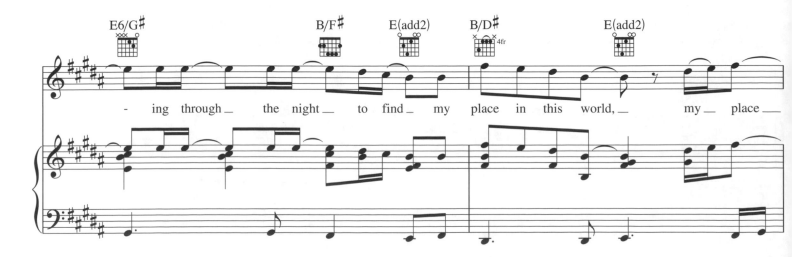

in this world. Not a lot to lean on. I need

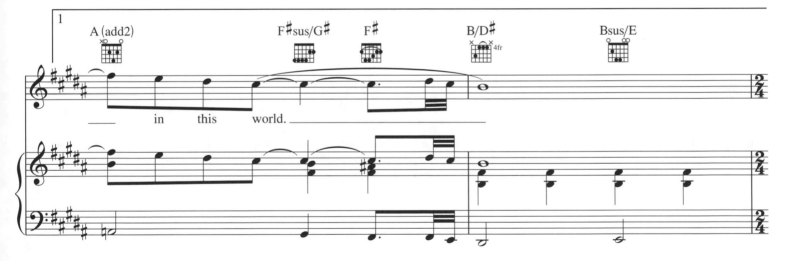

Your light to help me find my place in this world, my place

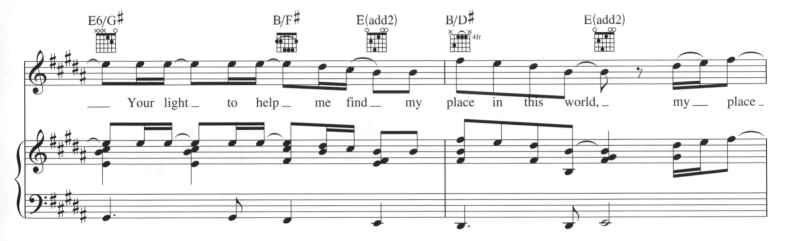

in this world.

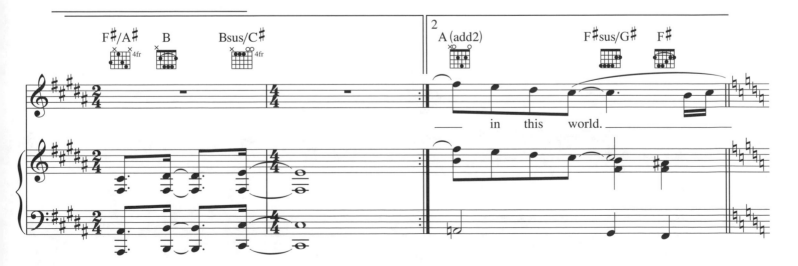

in this world.

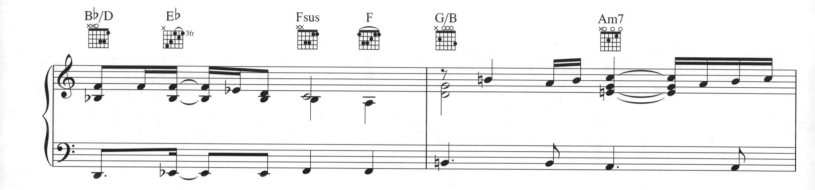

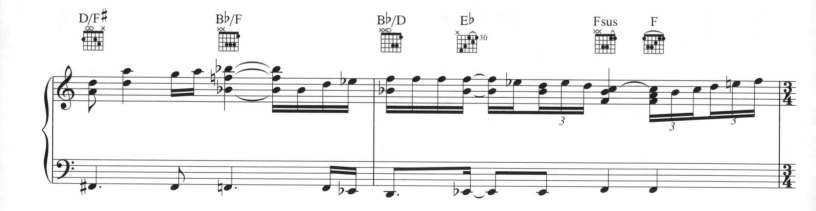

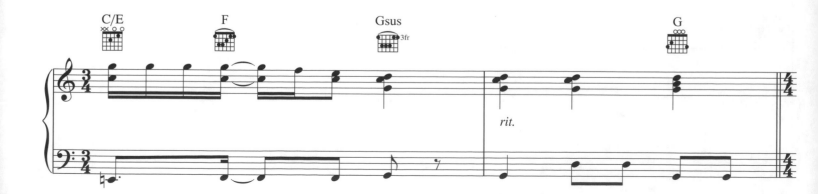

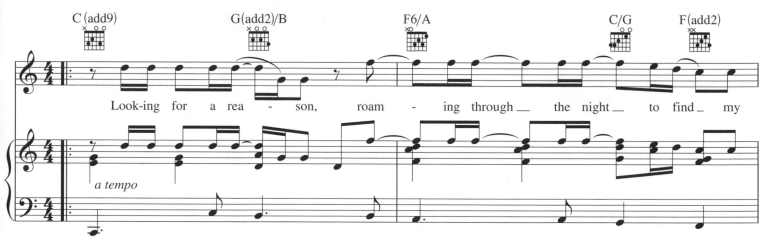

Look-ing for a rea - son, roam - ing through __ the night __ to find __ my

place in this world, __ my place _____ in this world. _____

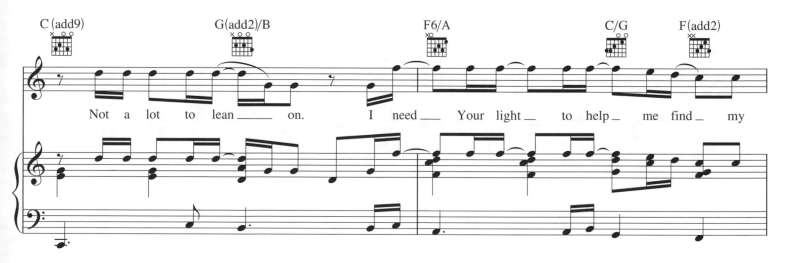

Not a lot to lean _____ on. I need ___ Your light __ to help __ me find __ my

Repeat and Fade | **Optional Ending**

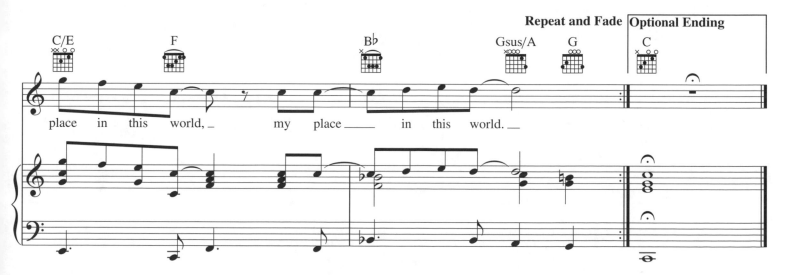

place in this world, _ my place _____ in this world. __

REVIVE US, O LORD

Words and Music by JON MOHR
and JOHN RANDALL DENNIS

Moderately slow

O Ho — ly God __ and King, __
Hum — bly, Lord, __ we now __ con — fess __

hear Your peo — ple as __ we sing. __ Re — vive us, O ____
wan — d'ring hearts __ and self — ish — ness. __ Re — vive us, O ____

Lord. _____
Lord. _____

Grant us this __ our one __ re — quest: __ that
We rec — og — nize __ our des — p'rate need __ for

Do, O Lord,__ what You__ must do__ to turn Your peo - ple's hearts__ to You.__ Re-

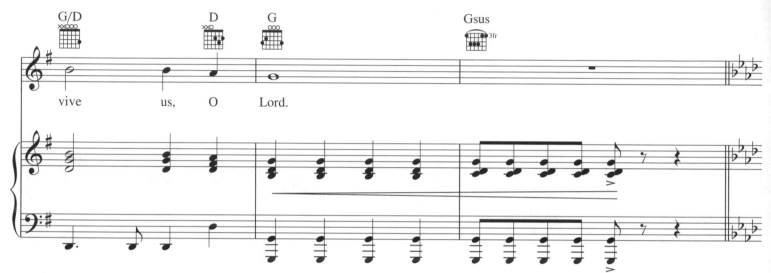

vive us, O Lord.

Fill us, Lord,__ this ver - y hour,__ in - fuse us with__ Your sa - cred pow'r.__ Re-

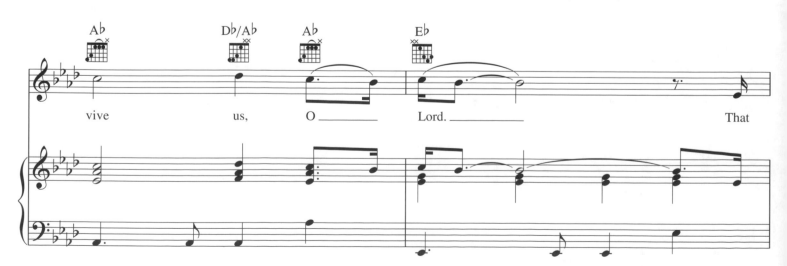

vive us, O_____ Lord._____ That

as Your peo - ple we _ might be _ all that You _ would have _ us be. _ Re-

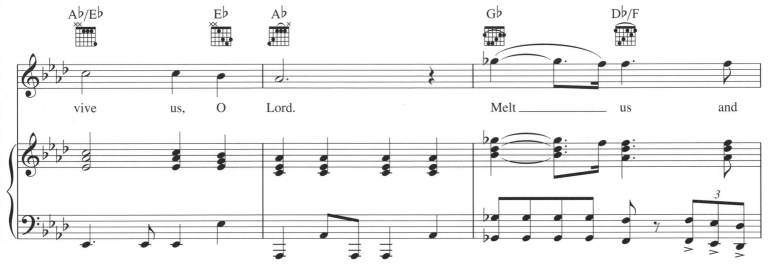

vive us, O Lord. Melt ___ us and

break _ us. _ Mold and re -

make ___ us. ___

Do, O Lord,__ what You__ must do __ to turn Your peo - ple's hearts__ to You.__ Re-

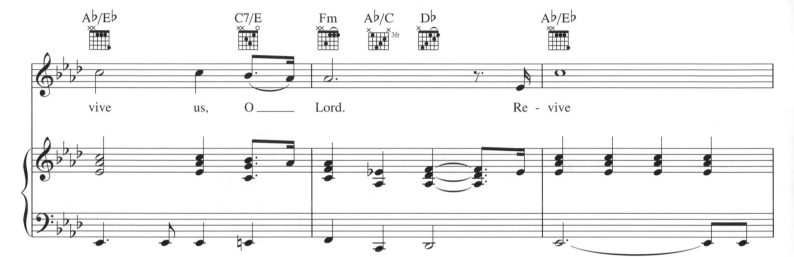

vive us, O ____ Lord. Re - vive

us, O Lord. _____

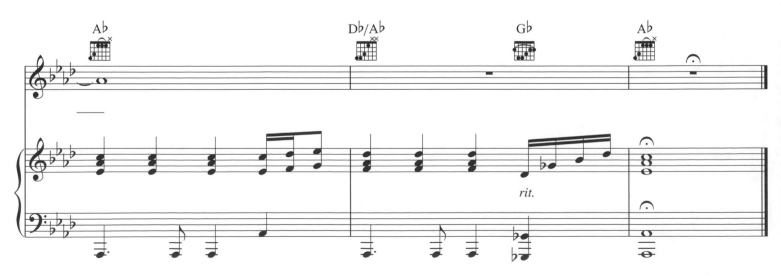

rit.

SING YOUR PRAISE TO THE LORD

Words and Music by
RICHARD MULLINS

With excitement

Recorded a half step lower.

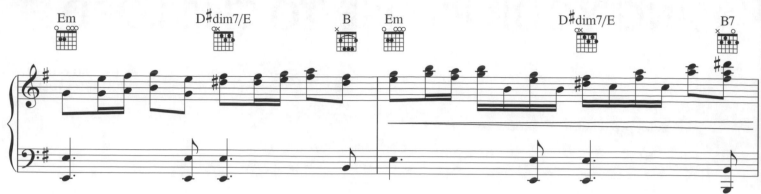

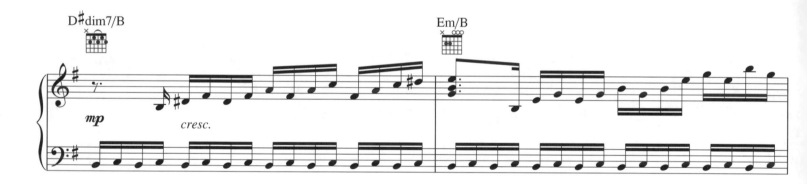

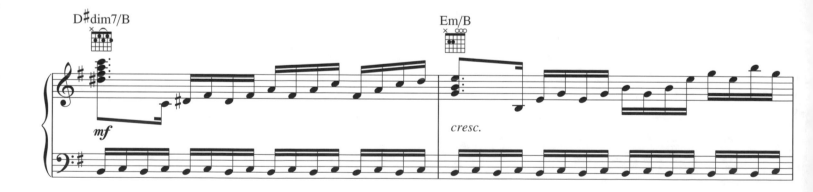

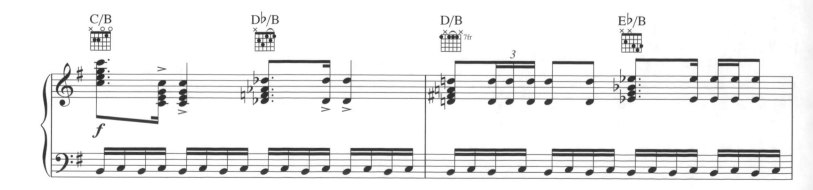

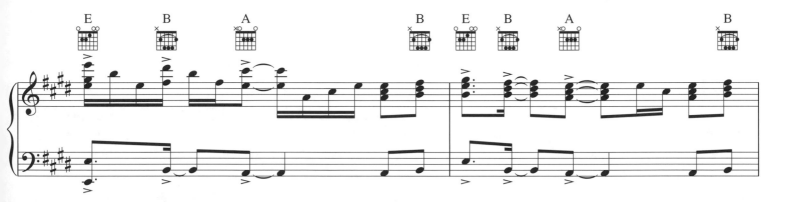

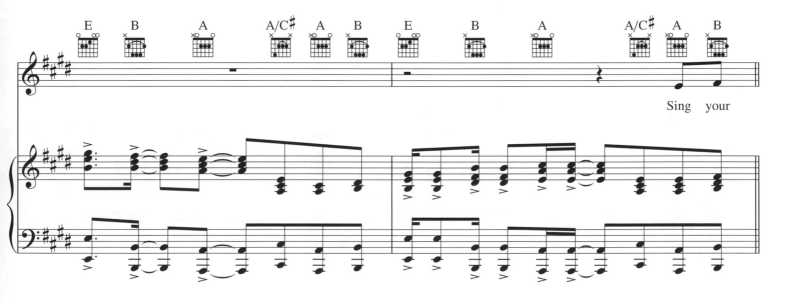

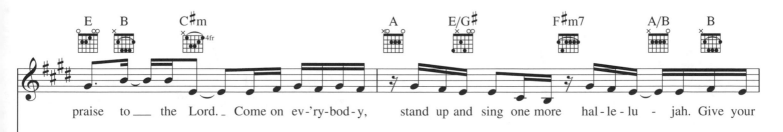

Sing your

praise to ___ the Lord. __ Come on ev-'ry-bod-y, stand up and sing one more hal-le-lu - jah. Give your

praise to __ the Lord. __ I can nev-er tell you just how much good that it's gon-na do __ ya just to

sing a - new the song your heart __ learned to sing when He __ first gave His

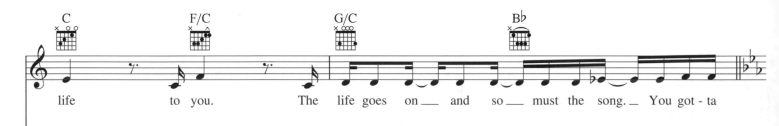

life to you. The life goes on __ and so __ must the song. __ You got - ta

sing a - gain the song born __ in your soul when you __ first gave your

praise to ___ the Lord. ___ I can nev - er tell you just how much good that it's gon - na do ___ ya just to

let the name of ___ the Lord ___ be praised both for now ___

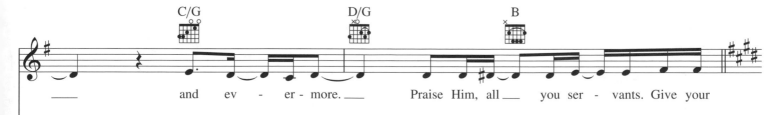

___ and ev - er - more. ___ Praise Him, all ___ you ser - vants. Give your

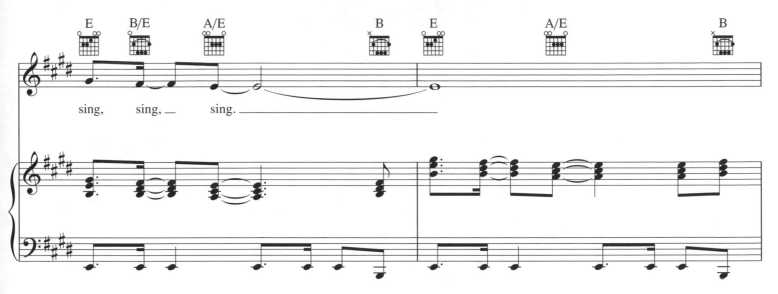

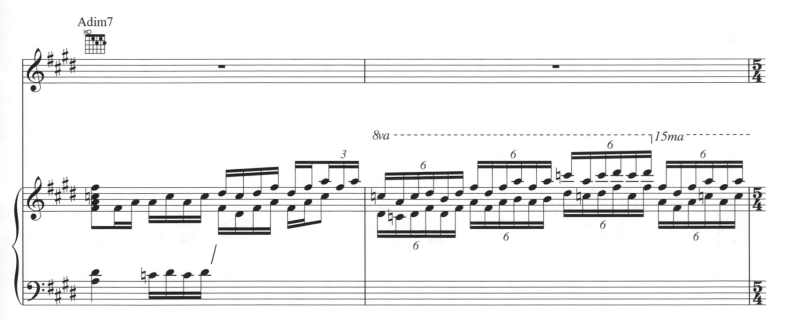

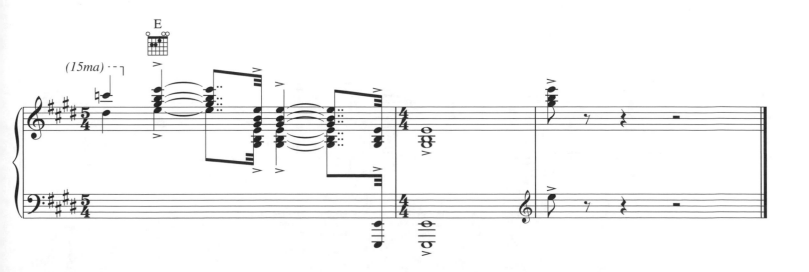

THE ROBE

Words and Music by WES KING
and PHIL NAISH

Moderately

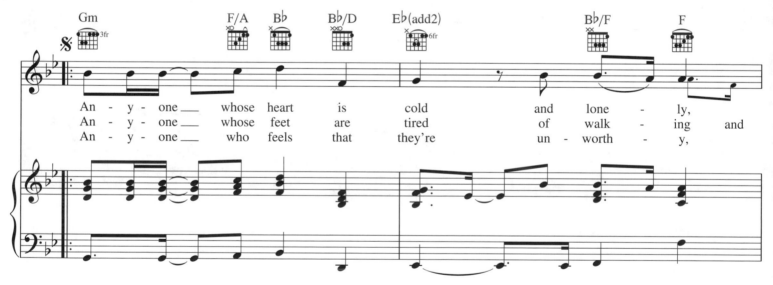

An - y - one ___ whose heart is cold and lone - ly,
An - y - one ___ whose feet are tired of walk - ing and
An - y - one ___ who feels that they're un - worth - y,

an - y - one ___ who can't be - lieve, _____ and
e - ven lost ___ their will to run, _____
an - y - one ___ who's just a - fraid, _____

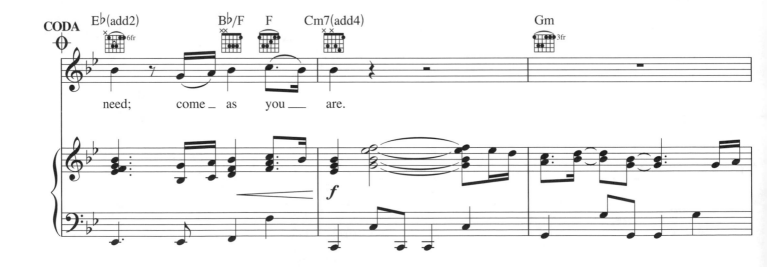

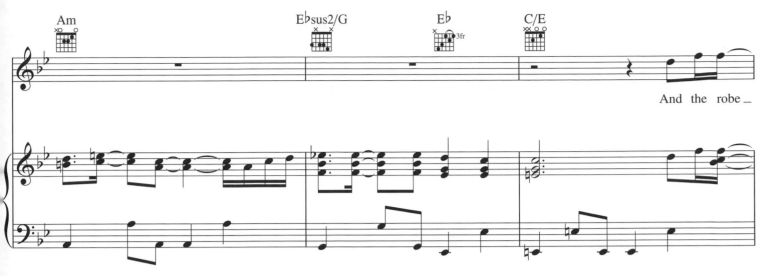

And the robe ___

___ is of God that will ___ clothe _____ your na - ked-

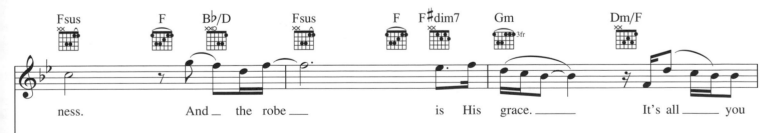

ness. And ___ the robe ___ is His grace. _____ It's all _____ you

dim.

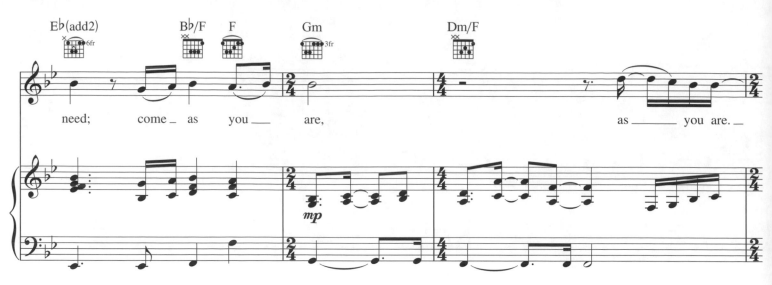

need; come _ as you _ are, as _ you are. _

_ Oh, it's all _ you need; _ come _

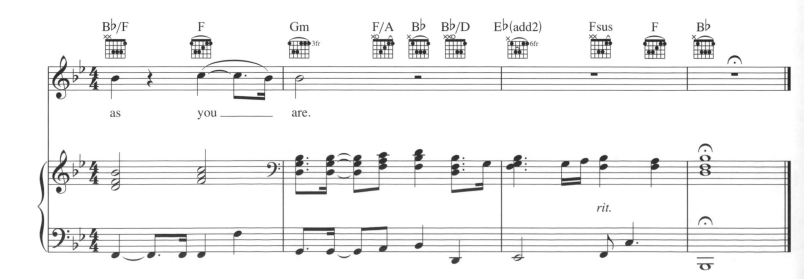

as you _ are.

rit.

SOMETIMES BY STEP

Words and Music by
DAVID "BEAKER" STRASSER

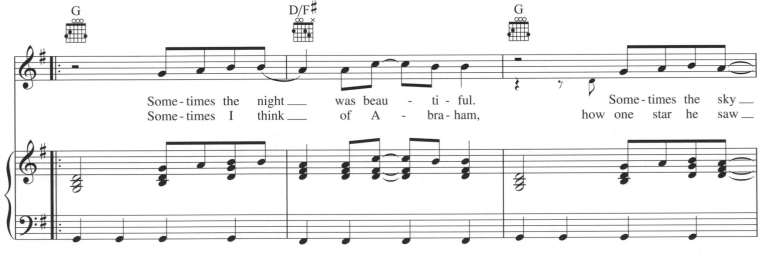

Some-times the night ___ was beau - ti - ful.
Some-times I think ___ of A - bra - ham,

Some-times the sky ___
how one star he saw ___

___ was so ___ far a - way.
___ had been lit ___ for me. ___

Some-times it seemed ___ to stoop ___ so close ___
He was a stran - ger in ___ this land, ___

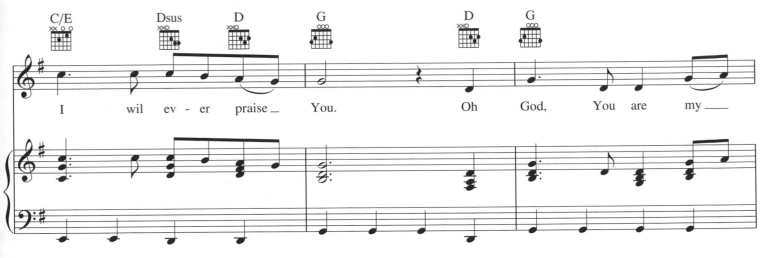

I wil ev - er praise _ You. Oh God, You are my _

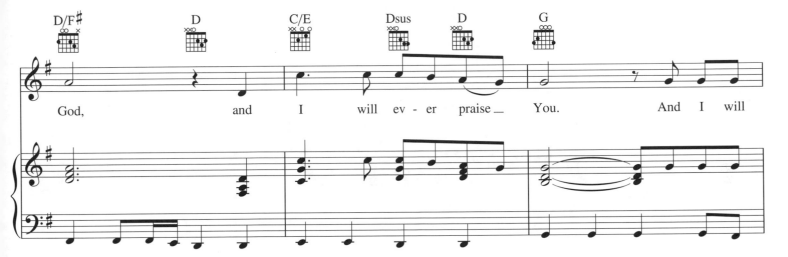

God, and I will ev - er praise _ You. And I will

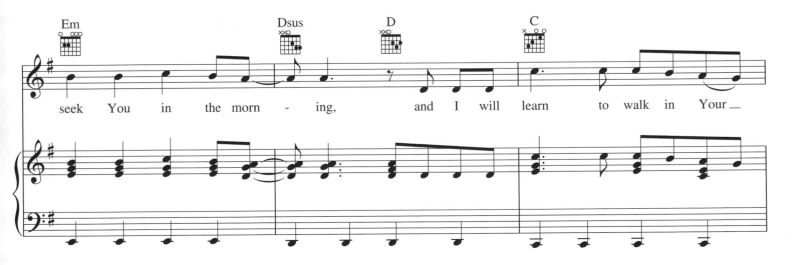

seek You in the morn - ing, and I will learn to walk in Your _

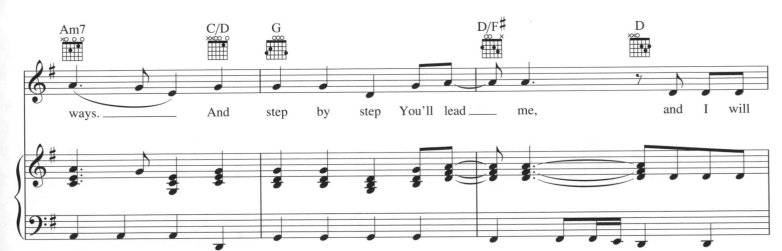

ways. _____ And step by step You'll lead ____ me, and I will

fol - low You all of my ___ days.

days. And I will fol - low You all of my ___ days, and I will

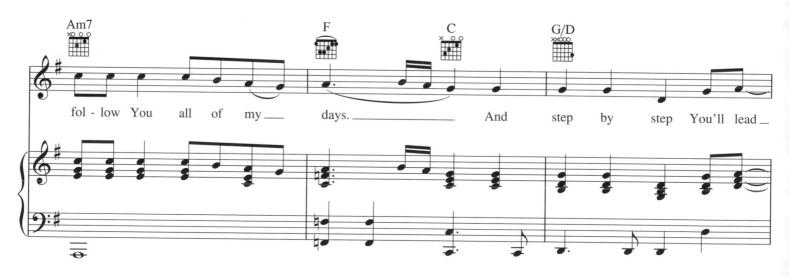

fol - low You all of my ___ days. _____ And step by step You'll lead ___

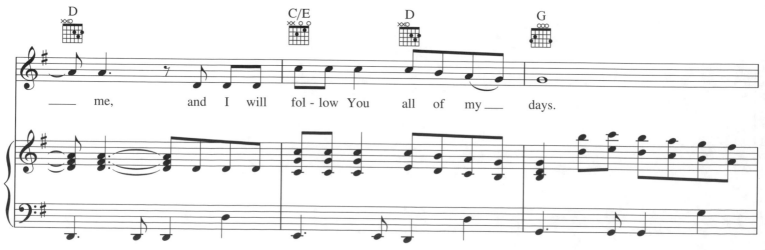

___ me, and I will fol - low You all of my ___ days.

And I will fol - low You all of my ___

days. And I will

Repeat and Fade

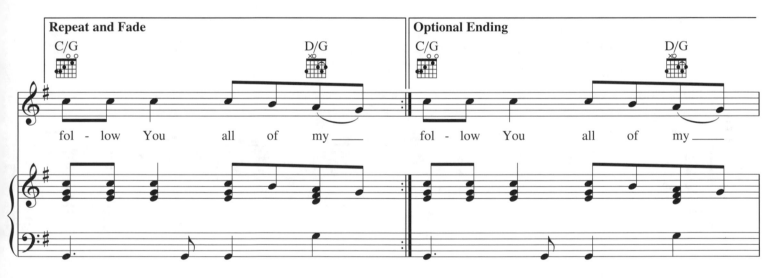

fol - low You all of my ___

Optional Ending

fol - low You all of my ___

days.

rit.

THIS IS YOUR TIME

Words and Music by MICHAEL W. SMITH
and WES KING

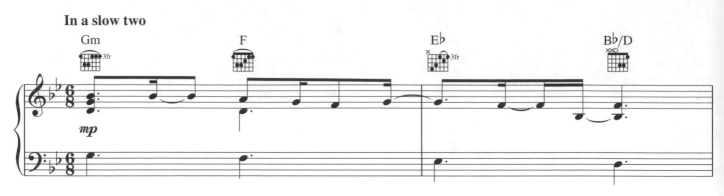

It was a test___ we could all___ hope to pass___ but none of us would want___
Though you are mourn-ing and griev-ing your loss,___ death died a long time___

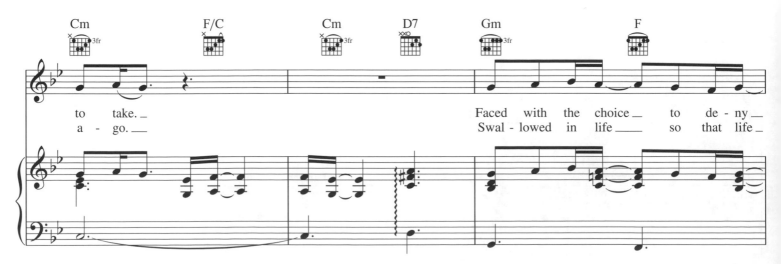

to take.___
a - go.___

Faced with the choice___ to de-ny___
Swal-lowed in life___ so that life___

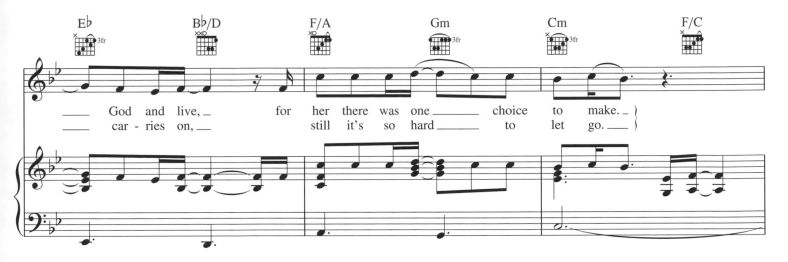

God and live, ___ for her there was one ___ choice to make. ___
car - ries on, ___ still it's so hard ___ to let go. ___

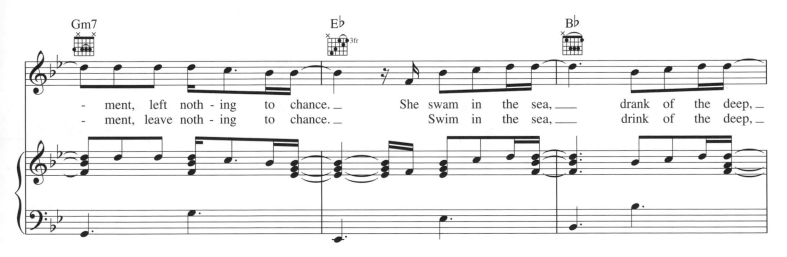

(1., 2.) This was her time, ___ this was her dance. ___ She lived ev - 'ry mo -
(D.S.) ___ this is your dance. ___ Live ev - 'ry mo -

- ment, left noth - ing to chance. ___ She swam in the sea, ___ drank of the deep, ___
- ment, leave noth - ing to chance. ___ Swim in the sea, ___ drink of the deep, ___

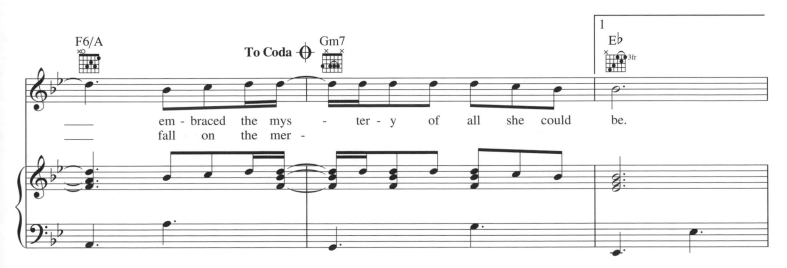

___ em - braced the mys - ter - y of all she could be.
___ fall on the mer -

This was her time.

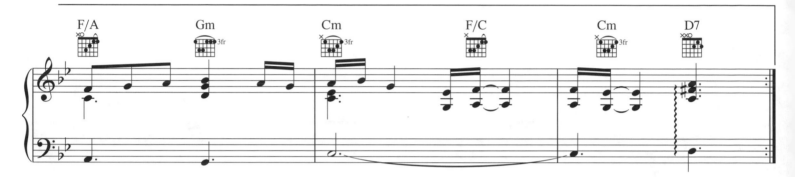

be. What if to-mor - row,___ and what if to - day?___ Faced with the ques-

- tion, oh, what ___ would you say? _____

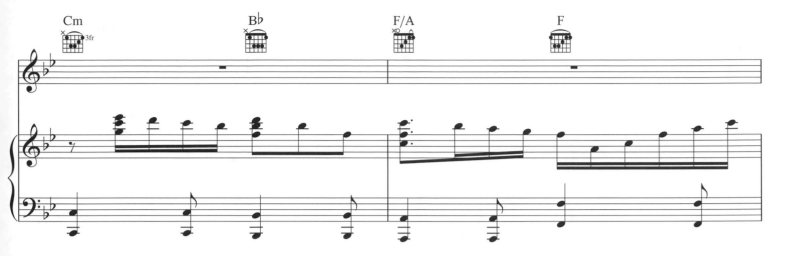

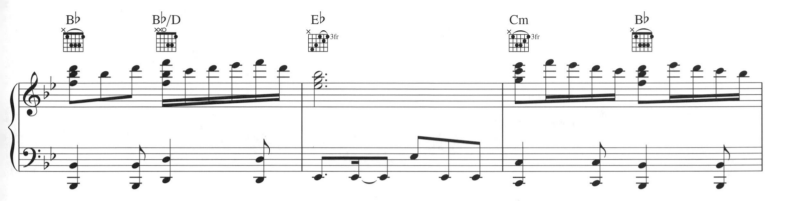

D.S. al Coda

This is your time, __

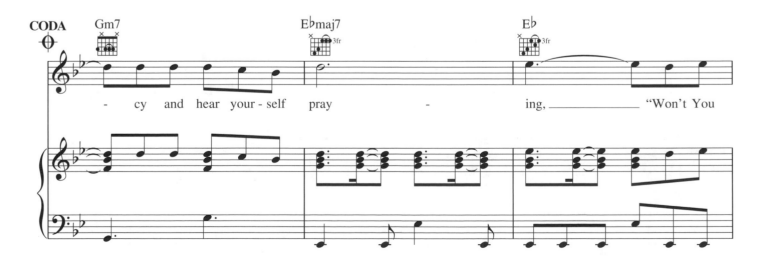

CODA

Gm7   Ebmaj7   Eb

- cy and hear your-self pray - ing, _____ "Won't You

save _____ me?

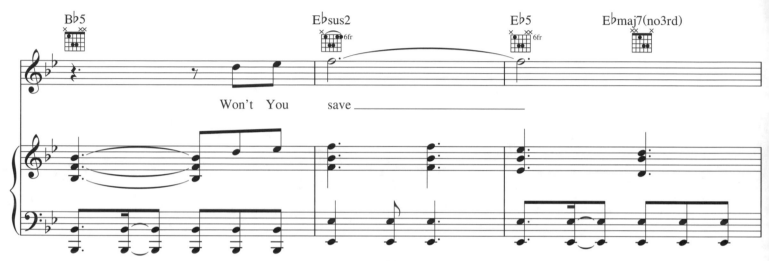

Won't You save _____

me?" This is your time, ___

___ this is your dance, ___ live ev-'ry mo - ment, leave noth-ing ___ to

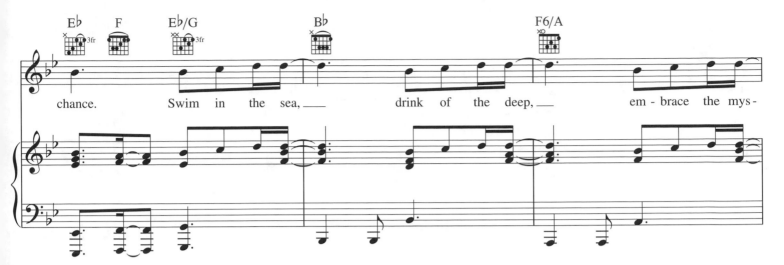

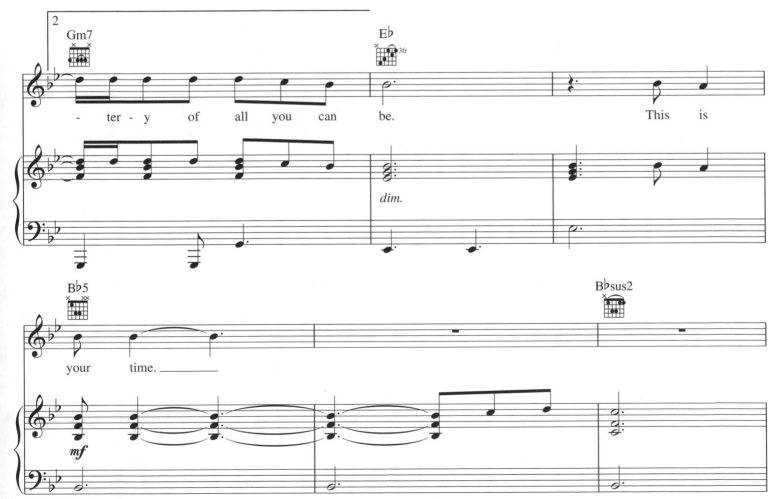

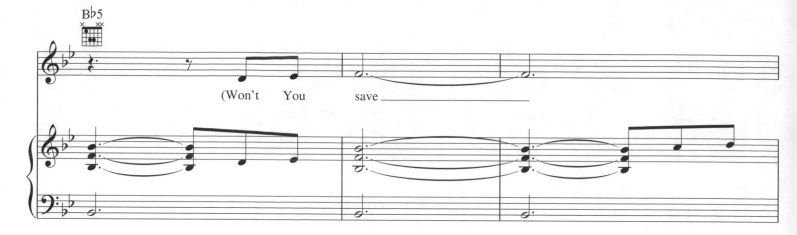

(Won't You save _____

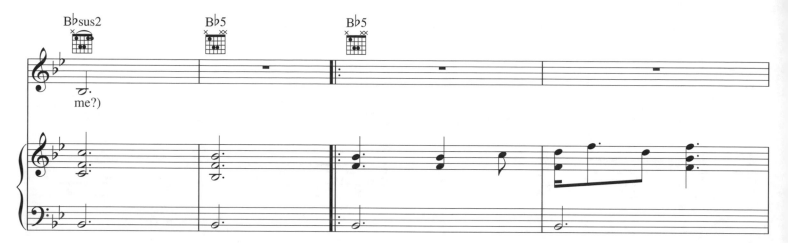

me?)

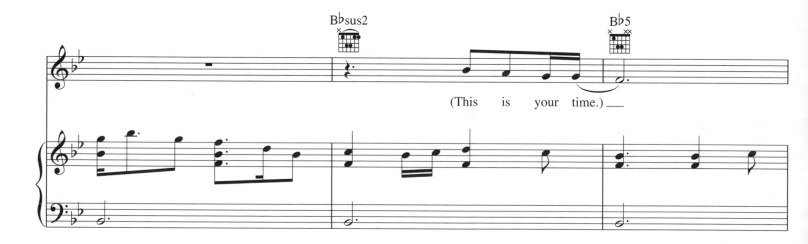

(This is your time.) ___

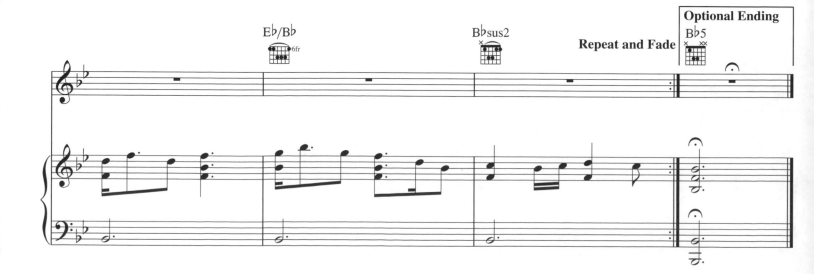

THY WORD

Words and Music by MICHAEL W. SMITH
and AMY GRANT

light _____ un - to _____ my path. Now

When I feel a - fraid, think I've lost __ my __ way,
I will not __ for - get Your __ love for me __ and __ yet my

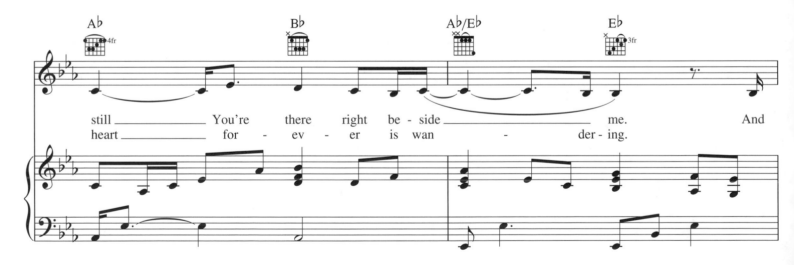

still _____ You're there right be - side _____ me. And
heart _____ for - ev - er is wan - der - ing.

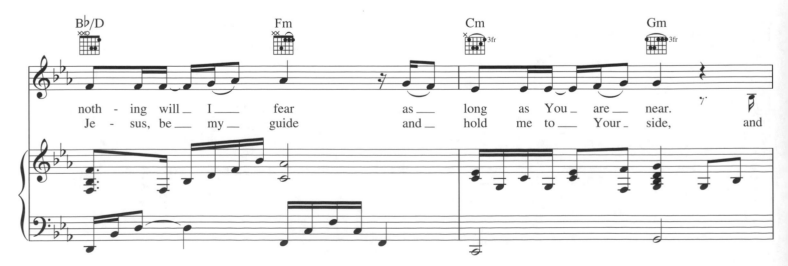

noth - ing will __ I __ fear as __ long as You __ are __ near.
Je - sus, be __ my __ guide and __ hold me to __ Your __ side, and

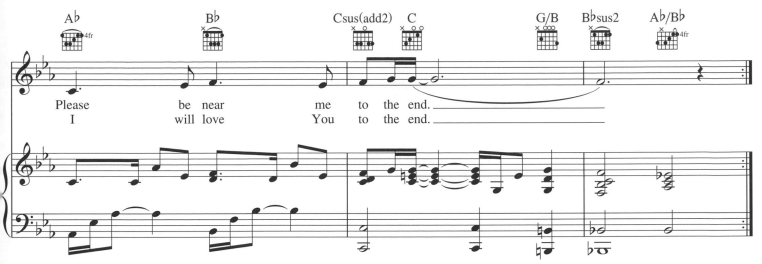

Please   be near   me   to the end. _____
I   will love   You to the end. _____

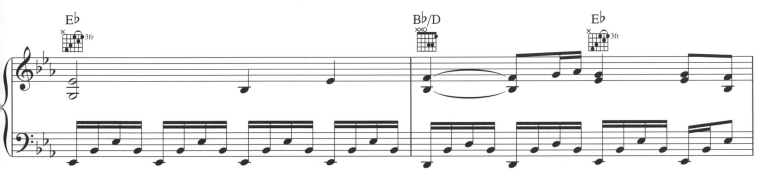

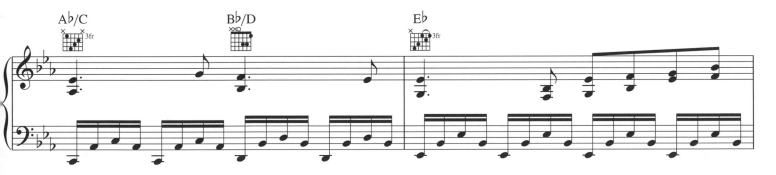

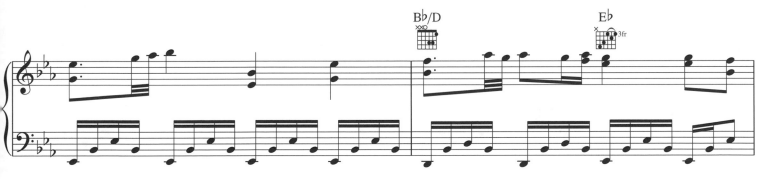

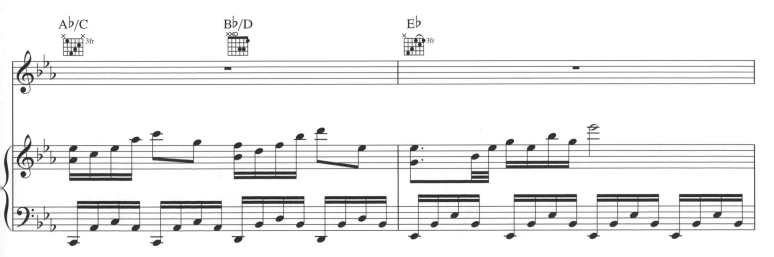

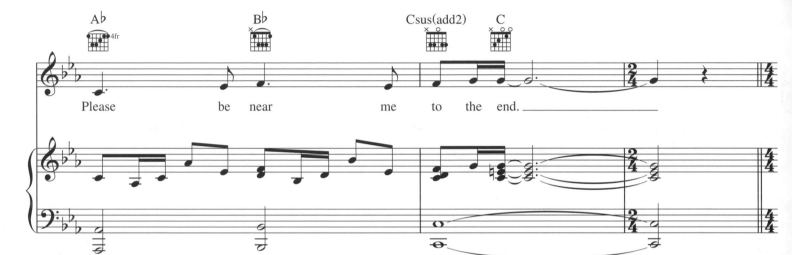

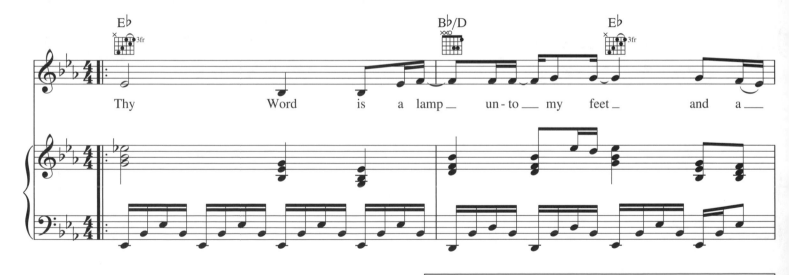

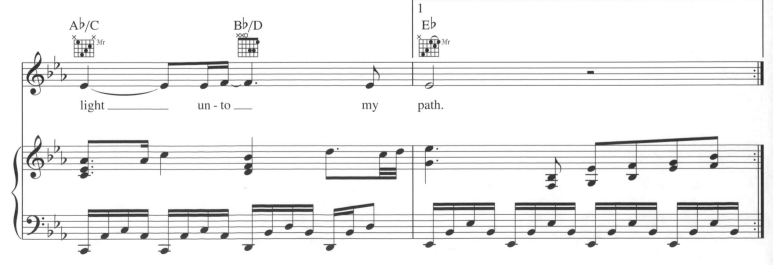

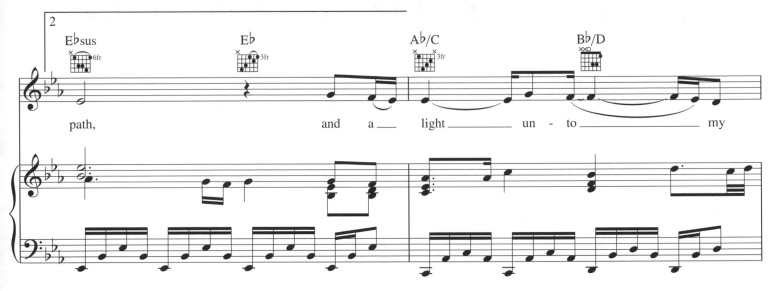

path, and a ___ light _____ un-to _____ my

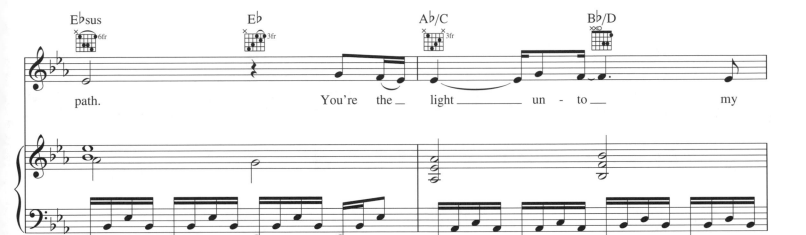

path. You're the ___ light _____ un-to ___ my

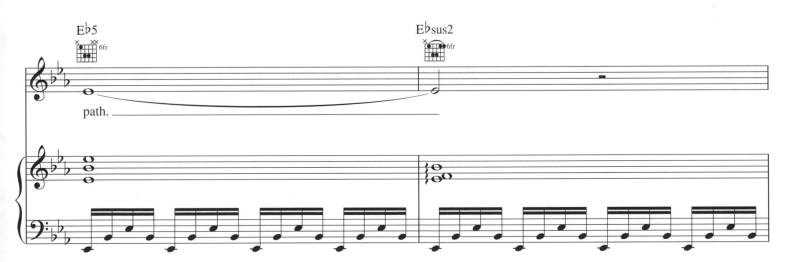

path. _____

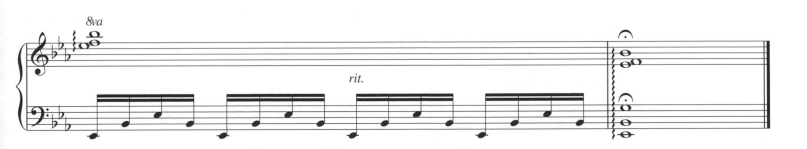

rit.

WAS IT A MORNING LIKE THIS?

Words and Music by
JIM CROEGAERT

Was it a morn-ing like this when the sun still hid from Je-ru-sa-

lem and Mar-y rose from her bed to tend the Lord she thought was dead?

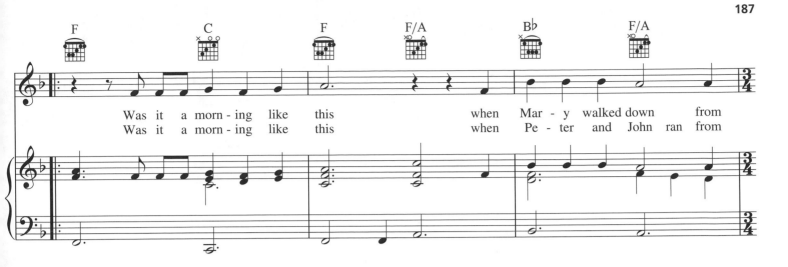

Was it a morn-ing like this when Mar-y walked down from
Was it a morn-ing like this when Pe-ter and John ran from

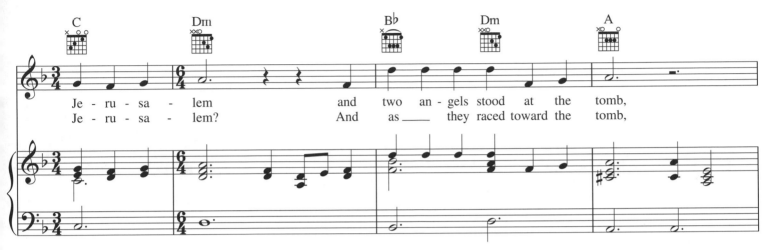

Je - ru - sa - lem and two an-gels stood at the tomb,
Je - ru - sa - lem? And as ____ they raced toward the tomb,

bear-ers of news she would hear soon? ____ Did the
be-neath their feet was there a tune? ____

grass sing? Did the earth re - joice to feel You a - gain? ____

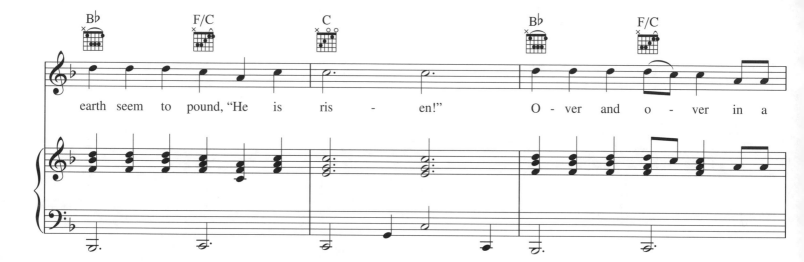

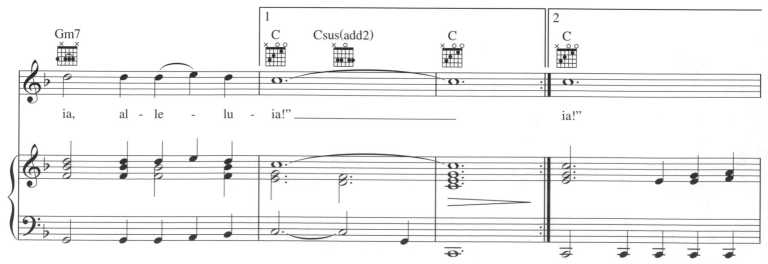

O-ver and o-ver like a trum-pet un-der-ground did the earth seem to pound, "He is

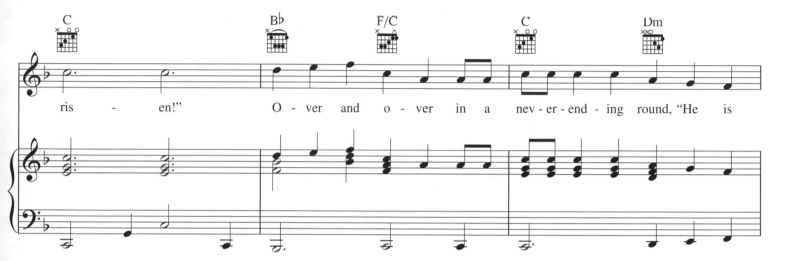

ris - en!" O-ver and o-ver in a nev-er-end-ing round, "He is

ris - en, al-le - lu - ia, al-le - lu -

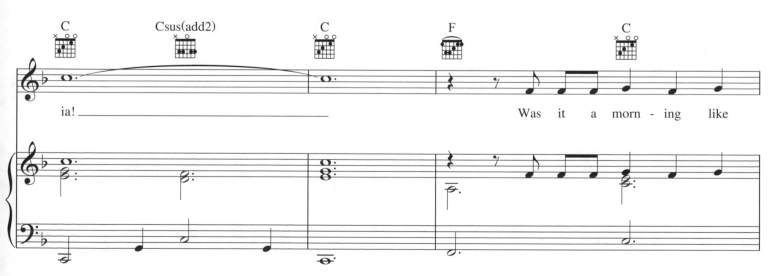

ia! _____ Was it a morn-ing like

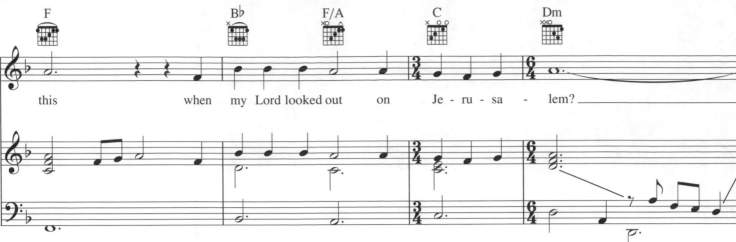

this   when my Lord looked out   on   Je - ru - sa - lem? _____

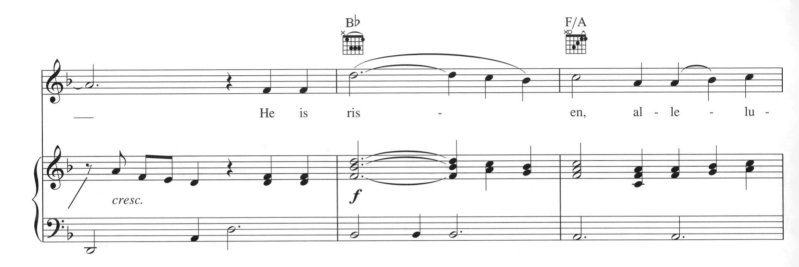

_____ He is ris - en, al - le - lu -

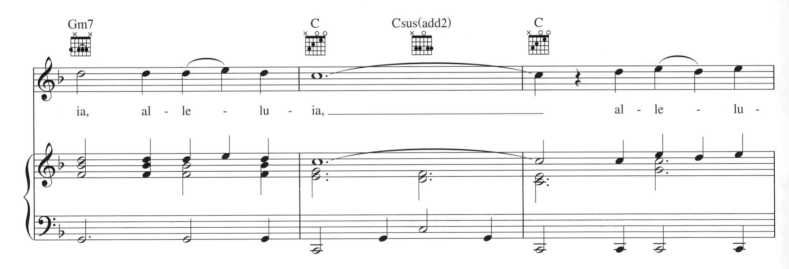

ia, al - le - lu - ia, _____ al - le - lu -

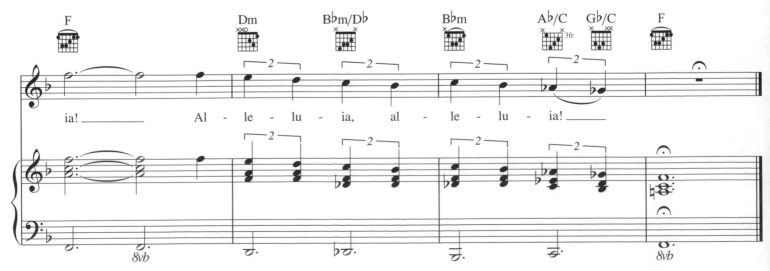

ia! _____ Al - le - lu - ia, al - le - lu - ia! _____

UNDIVIDED

Words and Music by
MELODIE TUNNEY

Moderately slow

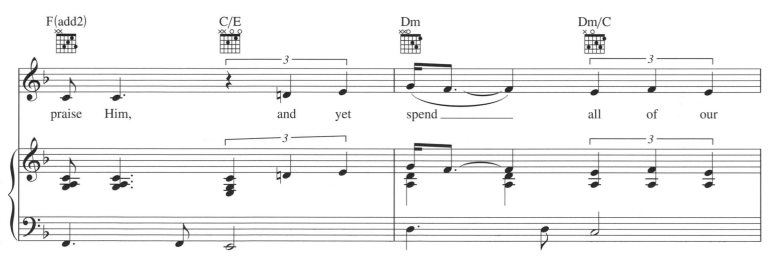

We __ may wor-ship dif-f'rent ways. We __ may

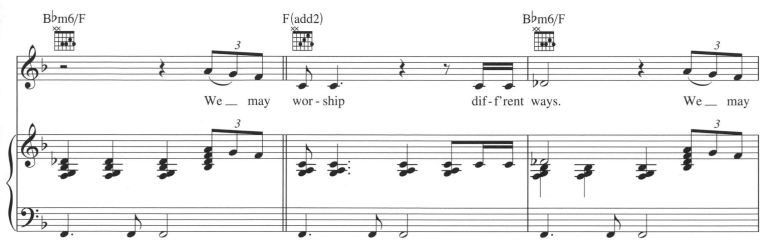

praise Him, and yet spend _____ all of our

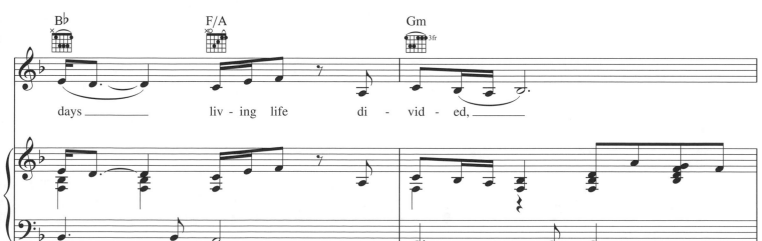

days _____ liv-ing life di-vid-ed, _____

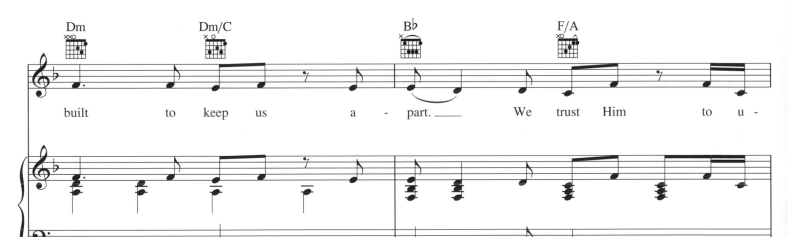

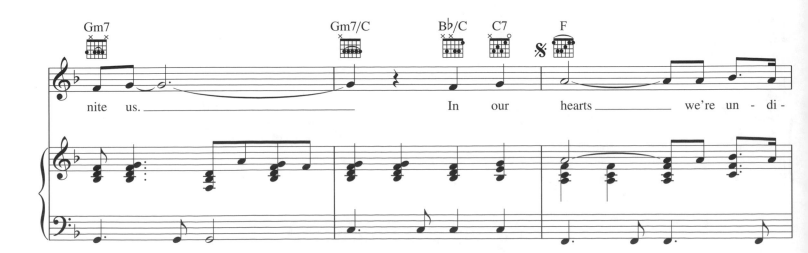

asks is that we _____ serve Him faith - ful - ly _____

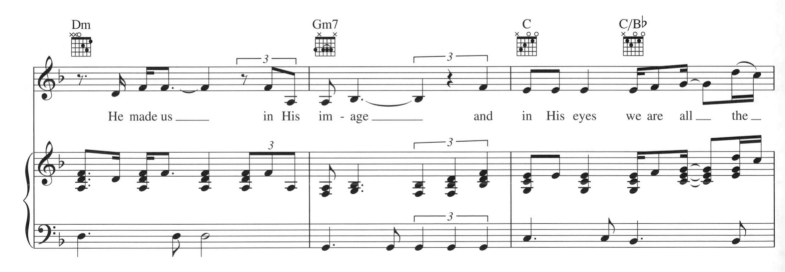

_____ and love _ as He first loved _ us. _____

He made us _____ in His im - age _____ and in His eyes we are all _ the _

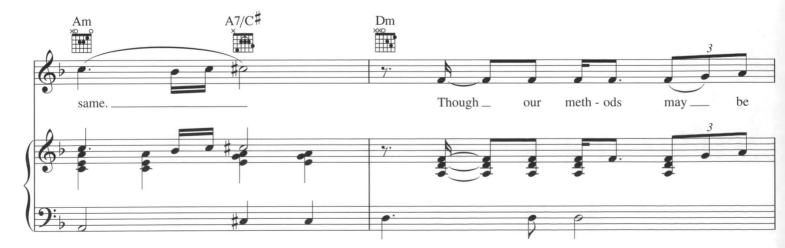

same. _____ Though _ our meth - ods may _ be

dif - f'rent, Je - sus is the bond that will re -

D.S. al Coda

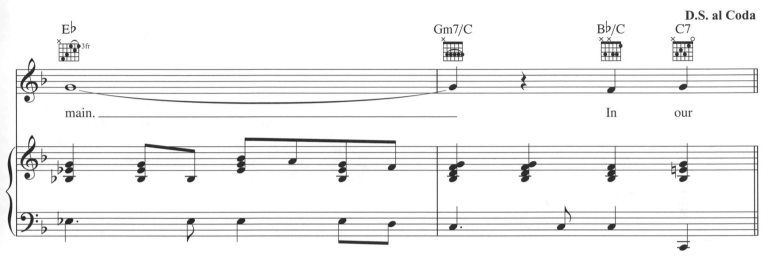

main. _____ In our

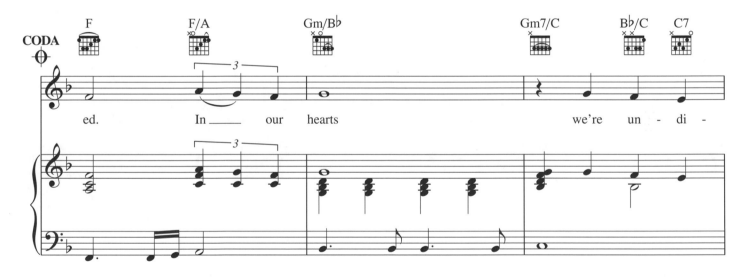

CODA

ed. In _____ our hearts we're un - di -

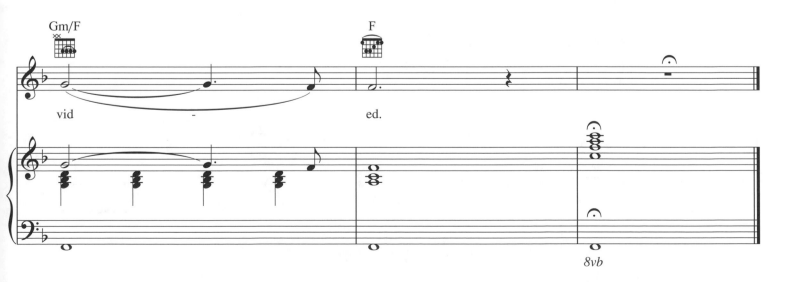

vid - ed.

8vb

WHERE THERE IS FAITH

Words and Music by
BILLY SIMON

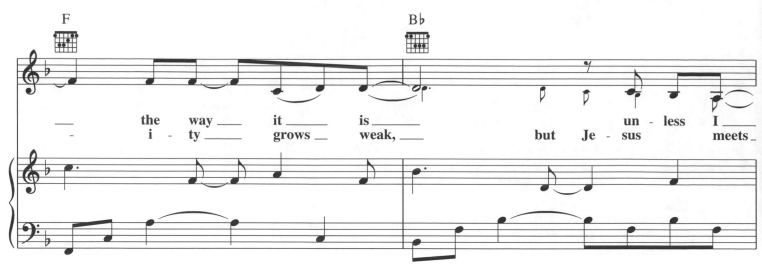

the way ___ it ___ is ___ but ___ un - less I ___
- i - ty ___ grows ___ weak, ___ but Je - sus I meets ___

___ be - lieve ___ that Je - sus lives. ___
___ our needs ___ if on - ly ___ we ___ be - lieve. ___

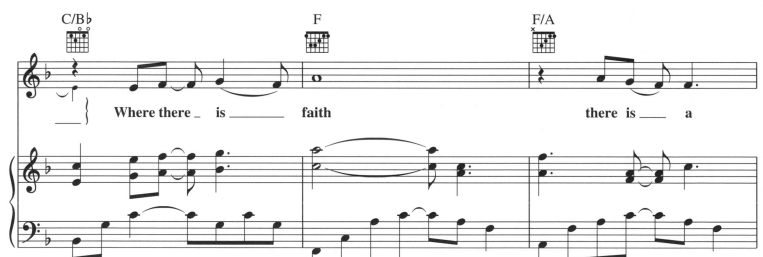

Where there ___ is ___ faith there is ___ a

voice call - ing; ___ keep walk - ing, you're not a -

WHO AM I

Words and Music by
MARK HALL

*Recorded a half step higher.

cause of what __ You've done. __ Not be - cause of what __ I've done, __

but be - cause of who __ You are, _____

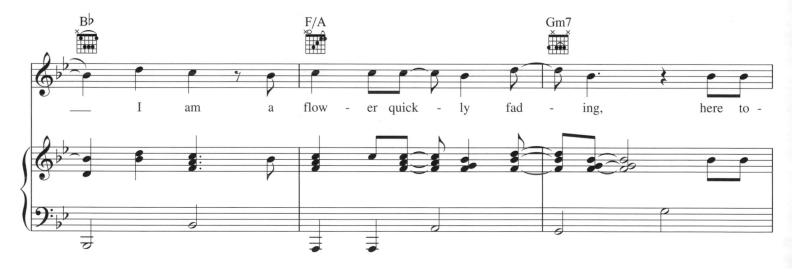

__ I am a flow - er quick - ly fad - ing, here to -

day and gone __ to - mor - row, a wave tossed __ in the o -

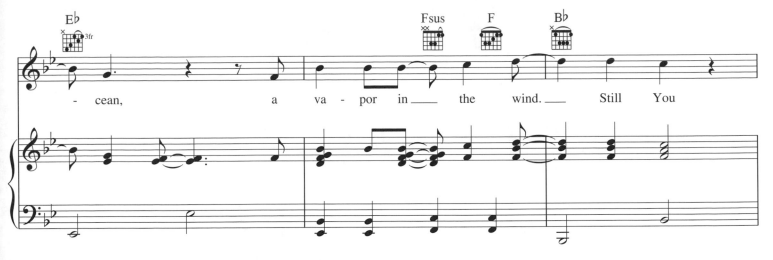

-cean, a va-por in ___ the wind. ___ Still You

hear me when ___ I'm call - ing. Lord, You catch me when ___ I'm fall -

To Coda ⊕

-ing and You've told me who ___ I am: ___

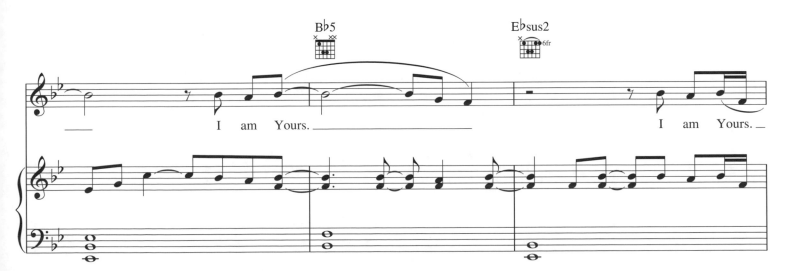

I am Yours. _____ I am Yours. ___

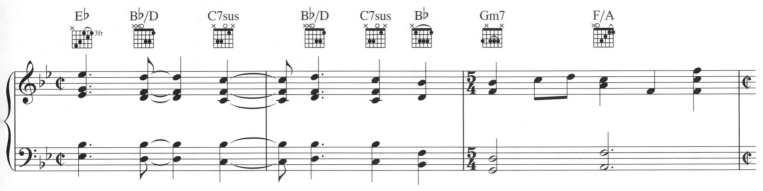

Not be - cause of who __ I am, _____ but be -

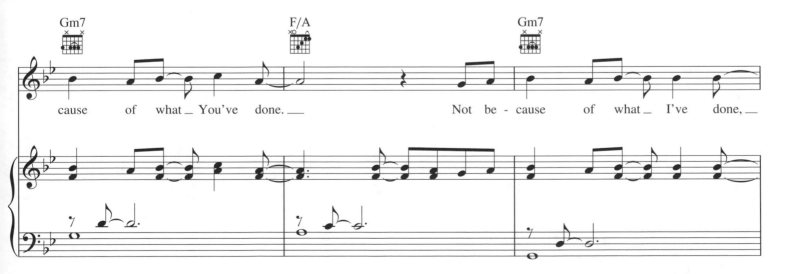

cause of what __ You've done. _____ Not be - cause of what __ I've done, __

but be-cause of who You are.

I am a flow-er quick-ly fad-

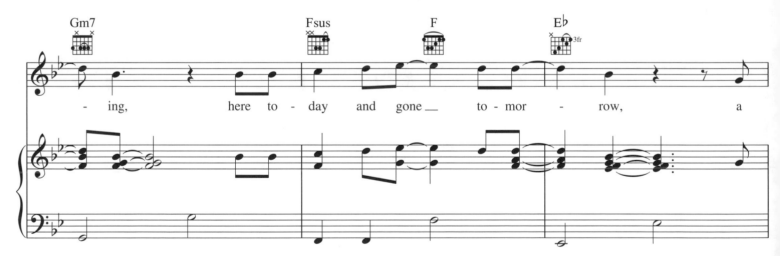

-ing, here to-day and gone to-mor-row, a

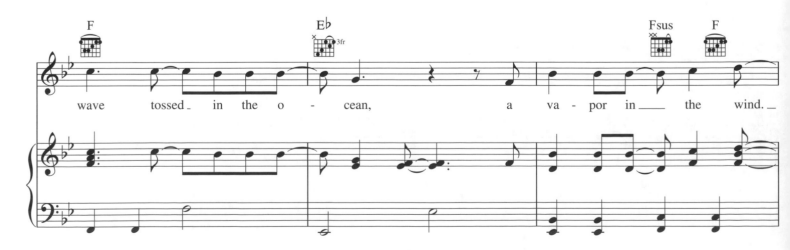

wave tossed in the o-cean, a va-por in the wind.

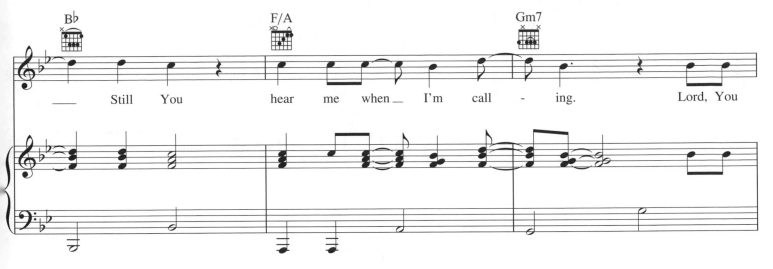

Still You hear me when __ I'm call - ing. Lord, You

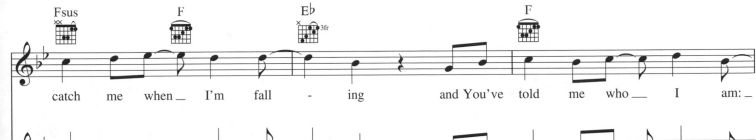

catch me when __ I'm fall - ing and You've told me who __ I am: __

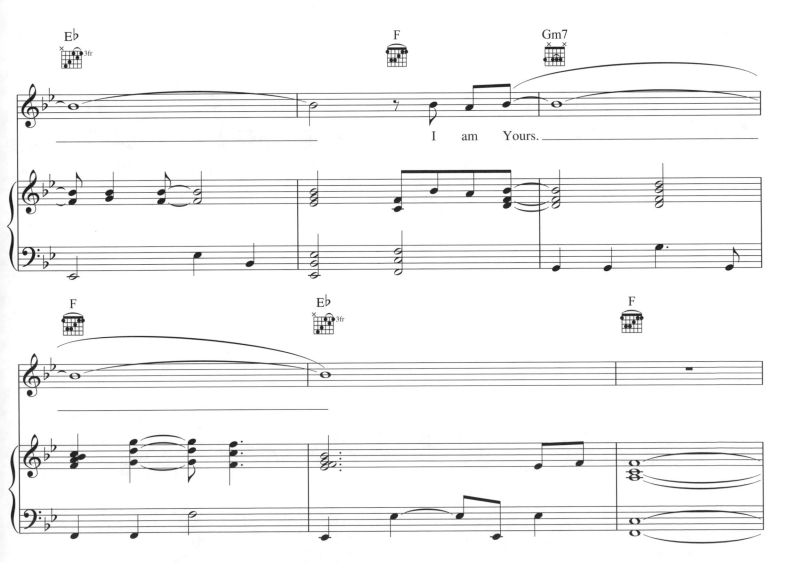

I am Yours. _____

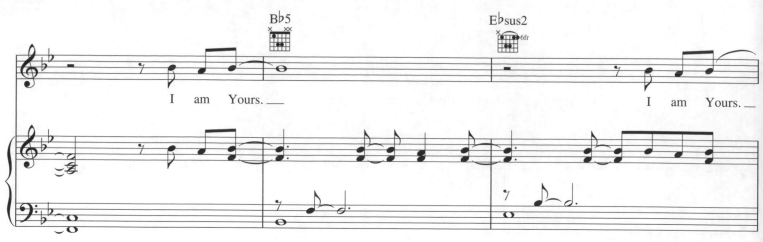

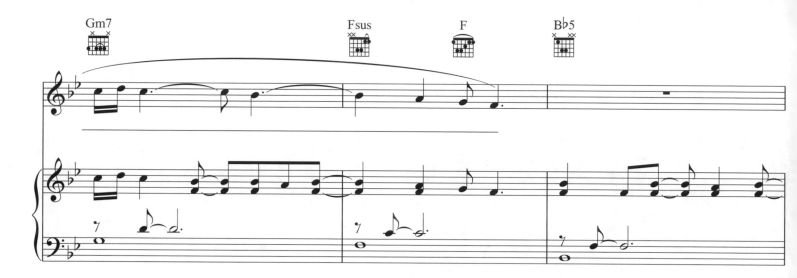

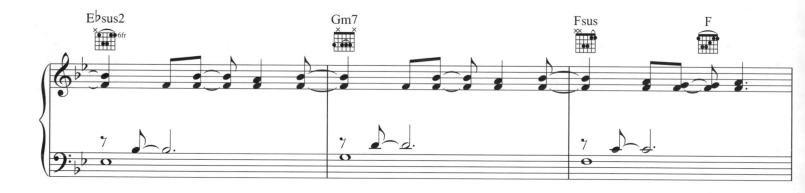

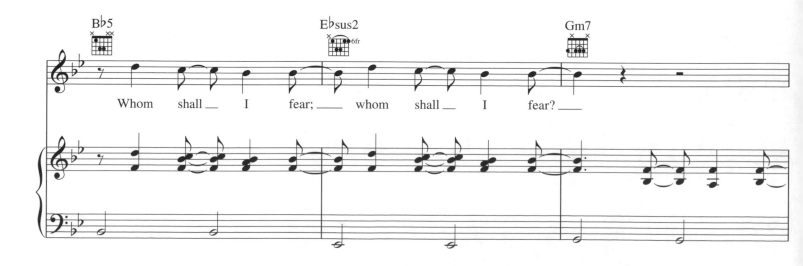

'Cause I _____ am Yours. _____

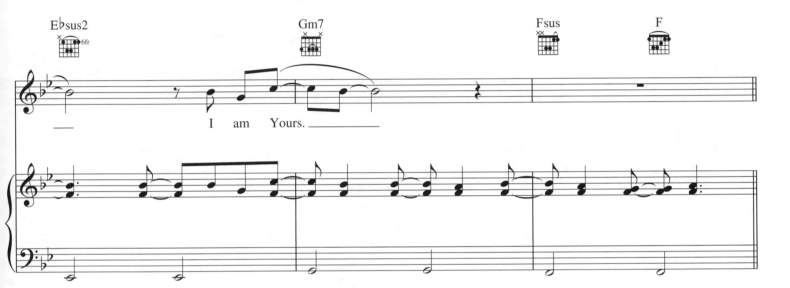

I am Yours. _____

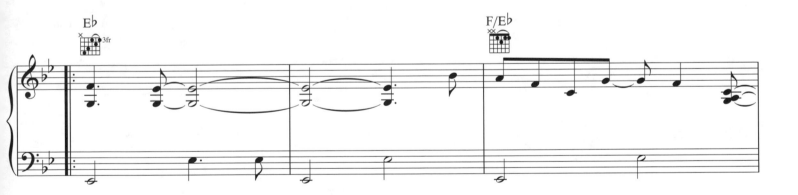

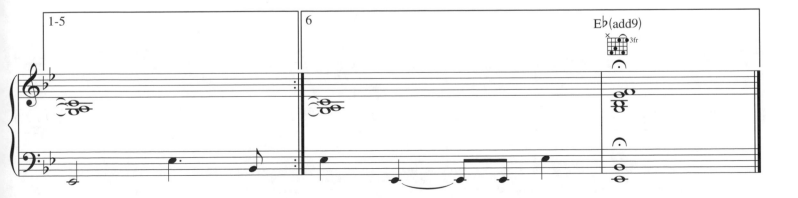

YOUR LOVE BROKE THROUGH

Words and Music by KEITH GREEN,
TODD FISHKIND and RANDY STONEHILL

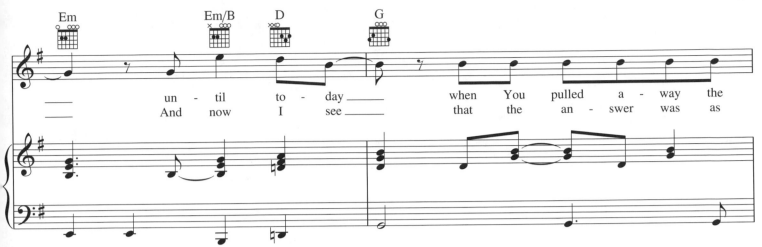

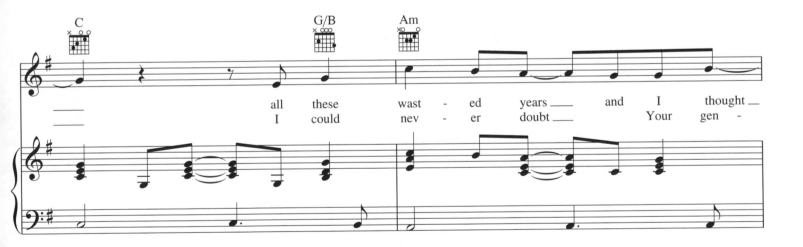

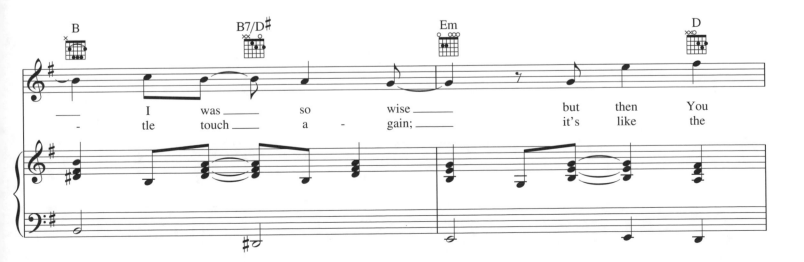

took me by ___ sur - prise. _____
pow - er of ___ the wind. _____

Like wak - in' up ___ from the long - est dream, ___

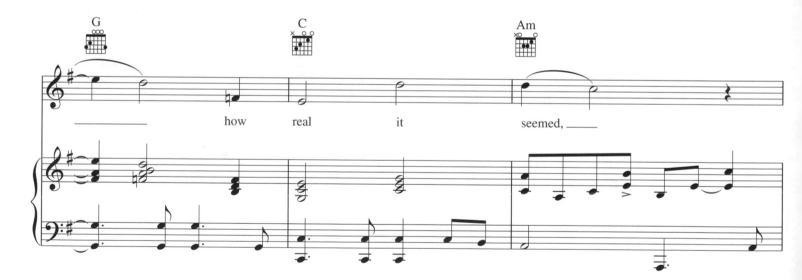

_____ how real it seemed, ___

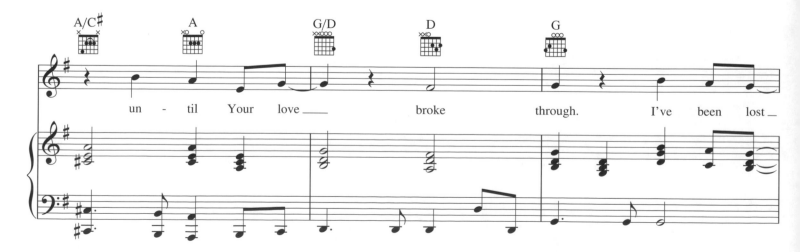

un - til Your love ___ broke through. I've been lost ___

in a fan - tas - y _____ that

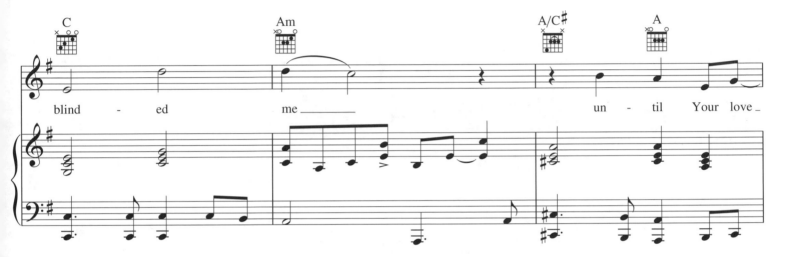

blind - ed me _____ un - til Your love _

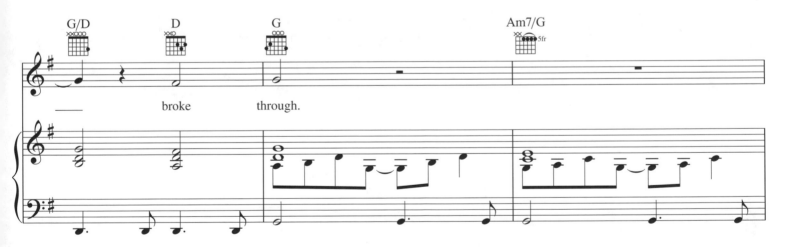

_____ broke through.

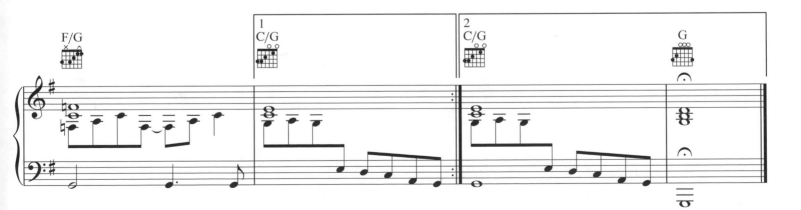

YOU RAISE ME UP

Words and Music by BRENDAN GRAHAM
and ROLF LOVLAND

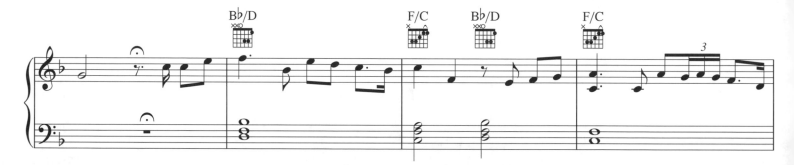

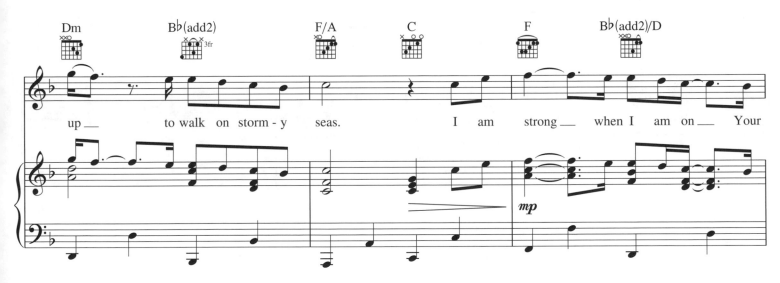

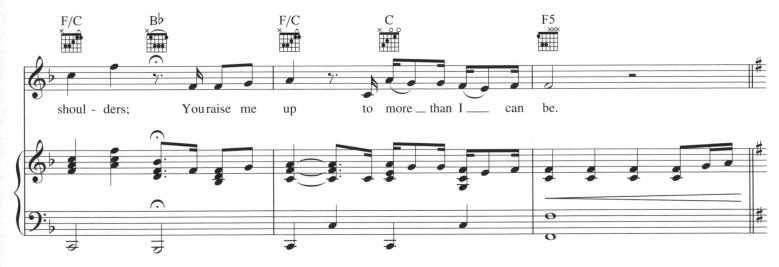

You raise me up _____ so I can stand on moun-tains; _____ You raise _ me

up _____ to walk on storm-y seas. I am strong _ when I am on _ Your

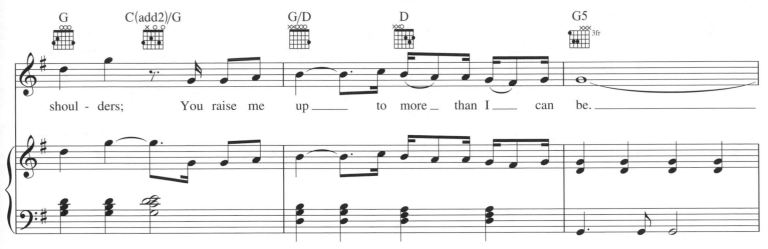

shoul - ders;   You raise me   up____   to more__   than I___   can   be.____

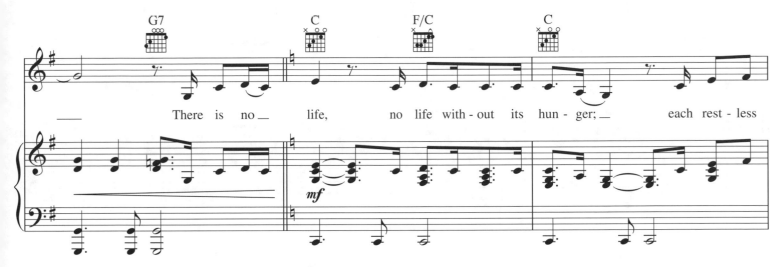

____   There is no___   life,   no life with - out   its   hun - ger;___   each rest - less

heart   beats so   im - per - fect - ly.   But when You   come___   and I   am filled with

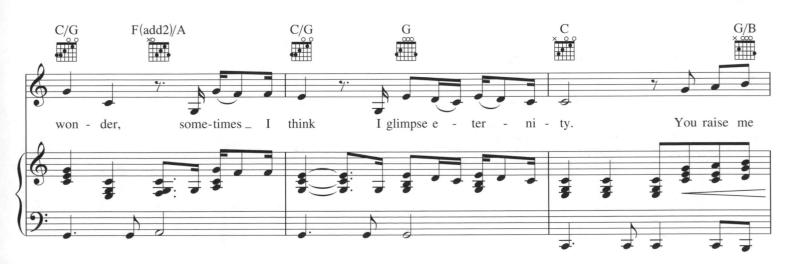

won - der,   some - times__ I   think   I glimpse e - ter - ni - ty.   You raise me

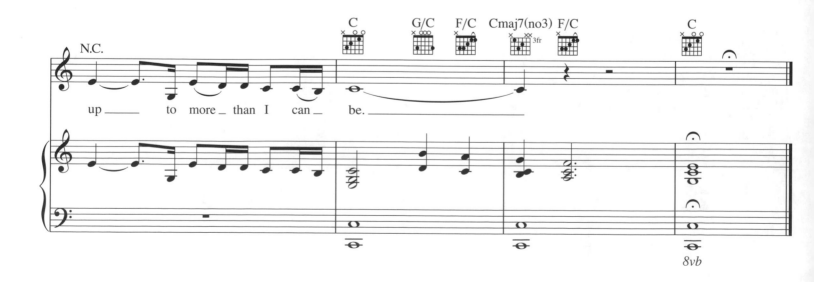

More Contemporary Christian Folios from Hal Leonard

Arranged for Piano, Voice and Guitar

AUDIO ADRENALINE – ADIOS: THE GREATEST HITS

17 of the best from one of the biggest successes in the CCM world. Includes: Big House • Chevette • Get Down • Some Kind of Zombie • Hands and Feet • Never Gonna Be as Big as Jesus • Ocean Floor • We're a Band • and more.

00306825 P/V/G $16.95

THE VERY BEST OF AVALON – TESTIFY TO LOVE

All 16 songs from the 2003 compilation by this acclaimed vocal quartet: Adonai • Can't Live a Day • Don't Save It All for Christmas Day • Everything to Me • Give It Up • Knockin' on Heaven's Door • New Day • Pray • Testify to Love • and more.

00306526 P/V/G $16.95

JEREMY CAMP – BEYOND MEASURE

This CD showcases Camp's powerful voice, which earned him back-to-back Male Vocalist of the Year GMA Music Awards. Our songbook features all 12 tracks, including the hit single "What It Means" and: Beyond Measure • Everything • Give Me Jesus • Let It Fade • Tonight • more.

00306854 P/V/G $16.95

CASTING CROWNS – LIFESONG

11 contemporary rock/worship songs from this popular band's 2005 album. Includes: And Now My Lifesong Sings • Does Anybody Hear Her • Father, Spirit, Jesus In Me • Lifesong • Love Them like Jesus • Praise You in This Storm • Prodigal • Set Me Free • Stained Glass Masquerade • While You Were Sleeping.

00306748 P/V/G $16.95

THE BEST OF STEVEN CURTIS CHAPMAN

21 songs from this award-winning Contemporary Christian/Gospel legend, including: Dive • The Great Adventure • Heaven in the Real World • Live Out Loud • Magnificent Obsession • More to This Life • No Better Place • Remembering You • and more.

00306811 P/V/G $17.95

DAVID CROWDER BAND COLLECTION

David Crowder's innovative alt-pop style has made him one of today's most popular worship leaders. This collection includes 16 of his best songs: Here Is Our King • No One like You • Open Skies • Our Love Is Loud • You Alone • and more.

00306776 P/V/G $16.95

STEVE GREEN – THE ULTIMATE COLLECTION

25 songs from the hits collection for this gospel star who got his start backing up Sandi Patti and the Gaither Vocal Band in the mid-'70s. Includes: Find Us Faithful • He Is Good • People Need the Lord • We Believe • What Wondrous Love Is This • and more.

00306784 P/V/G $19.95

KUTLESS – STRONG TOWER

The 2005 release by this Christian hard rock band hailing from Oregon includes 13 tracks: We Fall Down • Take Me In • Ready for You • Draw Me Close • Better Is One Day • I Lift My Eyes Up • Word of God Speak • Arms of Love • and more.

00306726 P/V/G $16.95

BRIAN LITTRELL – WELCOME HOME

Matching folio to the former Backstreet Boy's solo Contemporary Christian release. Includes all 10 tracks: Angels and Heroes • I'm Alive • My Answer Is You • We Lift You Up • Welcome Home (You) • and more.

00306830 P/V/G $16.95

Music Inspired by

THE CHRONICLES OF NARNIA

THE LION, THE WITCH AND THE WARDROBE

11 songs from the album featuring CCM artists. Includes: I Will Believe (Nichole Nordeman) • Lion (Rebecca St. James) • Remembering You (Steven Curtis Chapman) • Waiting for the World to Fall (Jars of Clay) • and more.

00313311 P/V/G $16.95

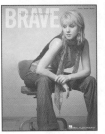

NICHOLE NORDEMAN – BRAVE

11 tracks from the 2005 album by this talented singer-songwriter: Brave • Crimson • Gotta Serve Somebody • Hold On • Lay It Down • Live • No More Chains • Real to Me • Someday • We Build • What If.

00306729 P/V/G $16.95

PHILLIPS, CRAIG & DEAN – THE ULTIMATE COLLECTION

31 of the greatest hits by this popular CCM trio. Includes: Crucified with Christ • Favorite Song of All • Here I Am to Worship • Lord, Let Your Glory Fall • Midnight Oil • Only You • Restoration • Shine on Us • This Is the Life • The Wonderful Cross • and more.

00306789 P/V/G $19.95

MICHAEL W. SMITH – GREATEST HITS

2ND EDITION

25 of the best songs from this popular Contemporary Christian singer/songwriter, includes: Friends • I Will Be Here for You • Place in This World • Secret Ambition • This Is Your Time • You Are Holy (Prince of Peace) • and more.

00358186 P/V/G $17.95

STARFIELD – BEAUTY IN THE BROKEN

Starfield wrote songs perfect for use in a modern church. Our matching folio to their 2006 release features all 11 tracks: Captivate • Everything Is Beautiful • Great Is the Lord • My Generation • Obsession • Unashamed • and more.

00306832 P/V/G $17.95

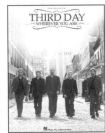

SWITCHFOOT – NOTHING IS SOUND

Switchfoot's rock style and street-smart faith has given them widespread success in CCM and secular arenas. This songbook from their 2005 release features 12 songs: Daisy • Happy Is a Yuppie Word • Lonely Nation • The Setting Sun • Stars • more.

00306756 P/V/G $16.95

THIRD DAY – WHEREVER YOU ARE

This popular rock band's 2005 release features "Cry Out to Jesus" plus: Carry My Cross • Communion • Eagles • How Do You Know • I Can Feel It • Keep on Shinin' • Love Heals Your Heart • Mountain of God • Rise Up • The Sun Is Shining • Tunnel.

00306766 P/V/G $16.95

CHRIS TOMLIN – ARRIVING

Our matching folio to the 2004 release from this award-winning singer/songwriter and worship leader from Texas features all 11 songs, including the hit singles: Holy Is Lord • How Great Is Our God • and Indescribable.

00306857 P/V/G $16.95

FOR MORE INFORMATION, SEE YOUR LOCAL MUSIC DEALER, OR WRITE TO:

HAL•LEONARD® CORPORATION

7777 W. BLUEMOUND RD. P.O. BOX 13819 MILWAUKEE, WI 53213

For a complete listing of the products we have available, Visit us online at **www.halleonard.com**

Prices, contents, and availability subject to change without notice.

0407

THE CHRISTIAN MUSICIAN

THE CHRISTIAN MUSICIAN series celebrates the many styles of music that make up the Christian faith. From Gospel favorites to today's hottest Christian artists, these books have something for all Christian musicians! There is no song duplication between any of the books!

CHRISTIAN ROCK

30 songs from today's hottest Contemporary Christian artists, including Audio Adrenaline, DC Talk, Delirious?, FFH, Jennifer Knapp, Jars of Clay, and Newsboys. Songs include: Consume Me • Everything • Flood • Get Down • Joy • One of These Days • Shine • Undo Me • and more.
00310953 Piano/Vocal/Guitar...........$16.95

CLASSIC CONTEMPORARY CHRISTIAN

30 favorites essential to all Christian music repertoire, including: Arise, My Love • Awesome God • Friends • The Great Divide • His Strength Is Perfect • Love in Any Language • People Need the Lord • Where There Is Faith • and more.
00310954 Piano/Vocal/Guitar...........$14.95

CLASSIC PRAISE & WORSHIP

Over 30 standards of the Praise & Worship movement, including: As the Deer • Great Is the Lord • He Is Exalted • Lord, I Lift Your Name on High • More Precious Than Silver • Oh Lord, You're Beautiful • Shine, Jesus, Shine • Step by Step • and more.
00310955 Piano/Vocal/Guitar...........$14.95

CONTEMPORARY CHRISTIAN HITS

30 of today's top Christian favorites, from artists such as Avalon, Steven Curtis Chapman, DC Talk, MercyMe, Nichole Nordeman, Point of Grace, Rebecca St. James, ZOEgirl, and others. Songs include: Always Have, Always Will • Between You and Me • Can't Live a Day • Dive • Fool for You • God Is God • I Can Only Imagine • If This World • If You Want Me To • A Little More • Live Out Loud • My Will • Run to You • Steady On • Testify to Love • Wait for Me • and more.
00310952 Piano/Vocal/Guitar...........$16.95

COUNTRY GOSPEL

Over 40 favorites, including: Church in the Wildwood • Crying in the Chapel • I Saw the Light • I Wouldn't Take Nothing for My Journey Now • Put Your Hand in the Hand • Turn Your Radio On • Will the Circle Be Unbroken • Wings of a Dove • and more.
00310961 Piano/Vocal/Guitar...........$14.95

GOSPEL'S FINEST

Over 40 Gospel greats, including: Because He Lives • The Day He Wore My Crown • Great Is Thy Faithfulness • How Great Thou Art • In the Garden • More Than Wonderful • Precious Lord, Take My Hand • Soon and Very Soon • There's Something About That Name • and more.
00310959 Piano/Vocal/Guitar...........$14.95

MODERN WORSHIP

Over 30 popular favorites of contemporary congregations, including: Above All • Ancient of Days • Breathe • The Heart of Worship • I Could Sing of Your Love Forever • It Is You • The Potter's Hand • Shout to the Lord • You Are My King (Amazing Love) • and more.
00310957 Piano/Vocal/Guitar...........$14.95

SONGS FOR A CHRISTIAN WEDDING

35 songs suitable for services or receptions, including: Answered Prayer • Celebrate You • Doubly Good to You • Faithful Friend • Go There with You • Household of Faith • I Will Be Here • If You Could See What I See • My Place Is with You • Parent's Prayer (Let Go of Two) • Shine on Us • 'Til the End of Time • Where There Is Love • and more.
00310960 Piano/Vocal/Guitar...........$16.95

SONGS OF FAITH FOR KIDS

50 favorites for kids of all ages! Includes: Arky, Arky • The B-I-B-L-E • Down in My Heart • God Is Bigger • He's Got the Whole World in His Hands • He's Still Workin' on Me • I'm in the Lord's Army • Lord, Be Glorified • Jesus Loves the Little Children • Salt and Light • This Little Light of Mine • Zacchaeus • and more.
00310958 Piano/Vocal/Guitar...........$14.95

FOR MORE INFORMATION,
SEE YOUR LOCAL MUSIC DEALER,
OR WRITE TO:

HAL•LEONARD®
CORPORATION
7777 W. BLUEMOUND RD. P.O. BOX 13819
MILWAUKEE, WISCONSIN 53213

Visit Hal Leonard Online at
www.halleonard.com

Prices, contents, and availability subject to change without notice.